CISTERCIAN FATHERS SERIES : NUMBER TWENTY

GILBERT OF HOYLAND

ON THE
SONG OF SONGS II

THE WORKS OF
GILBERT *of* HOYLAND

Translated and introduced by
LAWRENCE C. BRACELAND SJ

CISTERCIAN FATHERS SERIES: NUMBER TWENTY

Sermons on the Song of Songs, II

Cistercian Publications
www.cistercianpublications.org

LITURGICAL PRESS
Collegeville, Minnesota
www.litpress.org

A Cistercian Publications title published by Liturgical Press

Cistercian Publications
Editorial Offices
161 Grosvenor Street
Athens, Ohio 45701
www.cistercianpublications.org

The translation presented here is based on the edition of
Jean Mabillon, Milan, Gnocchi, reprint of 1852

Original Latin title:
Sermones in Canticum Salamonis ab eo loco ubi B. Bernardus morte praeventus desiit

The edition of Mabillon was checked against microfilm copies of two manuscripts: Paris 9605 in the Bibliothèque Nationale, of the twelfth century, from the monastery of Saint Victor, and Troyes 410 in the Bibliothèque Municipale, of the thirteenth century, from the monastery of Clairvaux, by the kind permission of the Librarians.

Where this edition of Mabillon shows some noteworthy difference from the edition of Migne, *Patres Latini*, 184, this is recorded in the notes.

This book has been published with the help of a grant from the Canadian Federation for the Humanities, using funds provided by the Social Sciences and Humanities Research Council of Canada.

Ecclesiastical permission to publish this work was granted by Bernard Flanagan, Bishop of Worcester.

© Cistercian Publications, Inc., 1979. © 2008 by Order of Saint Benedict, Collegeville, Minnesota. All rights reserved. No part of this book may be used or reproduced in any manner whatsoever, except brief quotations in reviews, without written permission of Liturgical Press, Saint John's Abbey, PO Box 7500, Collegeville, MN 56321-7500.

Volume II: ISBN 978-0-87907-632-0

Library of Congress Cataloging in Publication Data (Revised)

Gilbert, Abbot of Swineshead, Holland, Lincolnshire.
    Sermons on the Song of songs. (His The works of Gilbert of Hoyland ; v. 1–)
    (Cistercian fathers series ; no. 14, 20)
    Bibliography: p.
    Includes index.
    1. Bible. O.T. Song of Solomon—Criticism, interpretation, etc. I. Title.
    II. Series.
    BS1485.G49. 223'.9'066. 77-23026
    ISBN 0-8790-7414-0

CONTENTS

SERMON 16	Swordsmen on the border	203
SERMON 17	The rich carriage	217
SERMON 18	Purification, belief, vision, imitation	227
SERMON 19	Foundation and crown	237
SERMON 20	Affective contemplation	249
SERMON 21	Wonder over his two natures	263
SERMON 22	The eyes of a dove	273
SERMON 23	Discernment of spirits	283
SERMON 24	Understanding and affection	297
SERMON 25	Personal progress	305
SERMON 26	Battlements of the word and of charity	315
SERMON 27	Rapturous feast and the milk of babes	329
SERMON 28	The incense of prayer	341
SERMON 29	Invited to a crown	349
SERMON 30	Union of minds and hearts	361
SERMON 31	Milk of babes	373
SERMON 32	The Fragrance of the Anointed	385

Abbreviations 397

Monachis Dominae Nostrae in pascua peregrinantibus

Dominus regit me, et nihil mihi deerit:
in loco pascuae ibi me collocavit.
Super aquam refectionis educavit me,
Animam meam convertit.   Ps 22:1-3

SERMON 16
SWORDSMEN ON THE BORDER

His little bed is guarded by the sword of the word. 1. Christ is our Peacemaker and without him our labor is in vain; thanks to him peace abounds. 2. Peace was restored through Christ, but not yet are we without anxiety. 3. The spiritual require a strong guard, but should distinguish true and false bravery. 4. Some are skilled in the language of the court but not in the language of Scripture. 5. A man of the Gospel should speak the language of the Gospel. 6. The word of God should be a sword ready at his side. 7. Christ is the true Elisha and the true Elijah. 8. The spiritually weak must be cherished in the bosom of the Order until Christ raises a dead brother to life. 9. The little bed of Solomon surpasses all the little beds of the Saints.

THE LITTLE BED OF SOLOMON IS GUARDED BY SIXTY OF THE BRAVEST MEN OF ISRAEL, ALL EXPERTS WITH SWORDS AND VETERANS OF BATTLE, EACH WITH HIS SWORD AT HIS THIGH AGAINST ALARMS BY NIGHT.*[1]   *Sg 3:7-8

O how gracefully the bride ascends, almost without the burden of her body, wholly free from the flesh which decays! What bodily elements are hers, when she is compared to smoke? What seeds of decay, when that smoke coils up not from frail flesh but from burning incense? Gracefully she ascends, someone worthy of the bed of Solomon. I read that Esther bathed and anointed herself to charm the royal embraces with the fragrance of her ointments.* This bride, however, does not now use ointments to please her Bridegroom; she has herself been dissolved into the fragrance of ointments. But all do not understand this word;* all cannot enjoy these delights. If all shared the joy, all would be disappointed, whereas a pleasing variety and a devout charity is assured because while one shares the joy, another stands guard. The leisure of some is secure and joyful, because it is safeguarded by the watchfulness of others. Therefore 'the bed of Solomon is guarded by sixty of the bravest men of Israel'.

Our Solomon does not wish the tender delights of his bed to be disturbed or its affections to be lessened, let alone interrupted. He loves a peaceful realm, for he is styled the Peacemaker. Who is our Solomon but Jesus Christ? 'He himself is our peace, because he made both regions one people.'* He brought peace by his blood not only 'to everything on earth' but also 'to everything in heaven'.* 'The chastisement which brings us peace was laid upon him.'* He endured the chastisement we deserved, in order to pour upon us the peace of righteousness. He was punished; you were restored to grace.

You also were punished, but your travail could not beget peace for you. An unclean victim could not cleanse the defiled, not even itself, let alone others. Chastisement surely was inflicted on us but that chastisement was not for our peace. The sentence of death and suffering was passed on us but our unrighteousness was not dismissed. Indeed you were shackled at the decision of a judge but your guilt was not remitted. Punishment there was but peace there was not. O chastisement pitiful and severe, laid on the children of Adam! You crush without protecting, punish without purifying, consume without reconciling; you consume the substance of the flesh, not its guilt! What have you in common with peace?

Sermon Sixteen

When will you bestow peace, while you traffic with sin? When will you bestow grace, for you do not take away guilt? 'Indeed righteousness and peace have kissed each other.'*   *Ps 84:11. (Psalms follow the Vulgate enumeration.)*

'The chastisement which brought us peace' was laid upon him who brought us the peaceful harvest of righteousness.* He was called our only Solomon, our true Peacemaker,* because in his days righteousness has risen upon us and an overflow of peace.* Overflowing indeed is his peace. His peace not only sufficed to wash away the crimes of the past,* but will overflow forever. His peace overflows until the moon is no more,² until the labor of our mortal nature, changeable as the moon, is no more, until the labor of our defects, which wax and wane, is no more. Overflowing truly is his peace, for it was not meted out to match our merit. Merit, indeed, his peace did not find but conferred. How is that peace not overflowing, which both remitted the offence and added to the original grace? Peace was the possession of the first man in Paradise, so that he could not be led astray against his will; yet he did not possess the power by which he could afterwards be led back whenever he willed. He had grace enough to avoid an exit, but not the grace to reenter at will. Now there is more bountiful peace in the grace of Christ, which after repeated transgressions is freely offered. His peace does not banish but recalls the repentant. Overflowing surely is his peace, which cannot be dried up by any injury and is more ready to pardon than to punish. This peace, beginning with the forgiveness of sins, overflows even to the sharing of the divine nature, 'for one who clings' to God 'is one spirit with him'.*³

Heb 12:11
Col 1:20
Ps 71:7

Heb 2:17

2 P 1:4; 1 Co 6:17

2. You see how great is this fountain of expiation, so that it may at last be called not peace with God but rather union with him. O blessed border where the intervening wall of enmity has been removed! Blessed indeed is the enclosure, but not yet secure. Our enemy still attempts to cross its borders, to breach its walls. In Christ we possess peace with God the Father, but not yet peace with our common

enemy. Christ's peace, however, will overflow until the last personal enemy, death, is destroyed. In the meanwhile, even if there is no peace with the foe, there is protection against the foe. For Christ will be our peace, 'when the Assyrian comes into our land and sets foot' on our borders.* The Assyrian can infest the spiritual borders nearest to him but not those further away; he can trample upon but he cannot remain upon our borders. For Christ will be our peace when the Assyrian tramples upon our borders.

We have an inner border and an outer border; one with God and another with the world, a border with the spirit and a border with the flesh. And if to some persons it has been said: 'You are not in the flesh but in the spirit',* still they share a common border with the flesh, thanks either to the nature of their substance or to the care their flesh requires. The enemy then, using our flesh as his camp, from his vantage point infests the realm of the spirit and from his neighboring fortress plans his assaults. But 'he will be', yes, Christ will be 'our peace, when the Assyrian tramples on our borders'.* He is our Solomon, our peacemaker, who wins for us peace upon peace, peace with the Father, peace from the foe. He will 'win peace on our borders'.* O frontier and frontier, how much you differ from each other! With how many joys you overflow, O inner frontier; but to how many scandals you are open and subject, O frontier! O boundary and boundary! how gladly one of you is guarded but how laboriously the other is governed! On both sides Christ is the central boundary wall: for the outer border separating, for the inner border uniting; beginning from the outer border and perfecting to the inner border. 'For Wisdom reaches mightily' from this outer border to that inner border, there 'ordering all things harmoniously'.* That inner border is his little bed. Therefore of the valiant woman is it said: 'From afar and from the furthest borders is her value.'* 'It is her value' for which the bridegroom puts himself in the scales, against which he weighs himself, for which he prizes himself, with which his yearning is satisfied.⁴ What else is this but the embrace and the little bed of the bridegroom? That is the ultimate boundary beyond which his yearning cannot extend and our faculty is insufficient to comprehend. It is the border where you reach your own limit, where you are exhausted, when you begin to be another, wholly in Christ and Christ solely in you. O true peace and full peace, when from the kingdom of God scandals will be banished, where there will be no dread on our borders, when there will not be an inner and an outer border but one border only, the border named above: the border of alliance and conformity with God alone, a border enjoying the delights of his little bed and not depending on the sword.

3. But now, that the joys of his little bed—however limited they are—may not be disturbed, a strong guard is needed indeed. Therefore 'the bed of Solomon is surrounded by sixty of the bravest men of Israel'. Even in the Gospel you read: 'When a strong man fully armed guards his own court, his possessions are in peace.'* Here a more abundant guard is mentioned, because more abundant is the grace of his little bed than the grace of the court and care for his bride is greater than care for his goods. Again, I read of an angelic guard with a flaming sword set at the gate of Paradise.* Is the little bed of Solomon not a kind of paradise? 'Ours is a little bed of flowers.'* In Scripture, our Solomon is a flower of the field; he is the tree of life.* Truly such a little bed is a paradise of delights. Do you see how abounding delights are surrounded by a close guard? For 'the bed of Solomon is guarded by sixty of the bravest men in Israel'. I shall not say much now about the significance of this number, but it seems to denote those who excel in righteous deeds and in knowledge of the Law. They belong to the bravest in Israel, who are strong in faith, who are steadfast in faith and act manfully; they can do all things, but in him who strengthens them, Christ.*

He is perversely brave, who exalts himself against the knowledge of God,* who against that knowledge

Lk 11:21

Gn 3:24
Sg 1:15

Sg 2:1; Pr 3:18

Ph 14:3

2 Co 10:5

is unbending and stubborn, whose strength is the strength of boulders and whose heart is of bronze, so that not even hammering brings understanding to his hearing. Such are those to whom Paul says: 'Are we provoking the Lord to anger? Are we stronger than he?'* He does not belong to the bravest in Israel, who when he is wounded feels no pain, when he is scourged is insensitive, who remains impervious to all the thrusts of the two-edged sword of the incisive word* and takes pride in kicking against the goads of wisdom.* Not such was Mary, whose soul, like softest material, the sword transfixed.* As for me, would that a valiant word might easily reach me; would that its incisiveness might work through me. Would that this sword might pierce my soul, that my soul also might be turned into a sword to fight against the spiritual powers of evil.*

1 Co 10:22

Heb 4:12
Ac 9:5
Lk 2:35

Eph 6:12; Lam 180, n. 66.

4. Why set your hand to deeds of bravery, you who are not one of the bravest? Why join the guard, when you do not shake off your lethargy? Why stand guard by the bed, when you have no sword, or if you possess the sword of the word, keep it on its page,5 not on your tongue? You do not hold in the grasp of your tongue the versatile sword of God's word. God's word is fluent, his spirit is fiery, but somehow, contrary to its nature, it becomes sluggish in your grasp. There it is sheathed and blunted, though it is sharper and more penetrating than any two-edged sword.* In your mouth the word is not quick, it does not flow quickly; in your grasp it is not versatile to suit the occasion, though in itself it is more than a match for any engagement in spiritual combat. Why usurp an office when you have no experience? The guards are 'all expert with swords and veterans of battle'.* Without reason do you bear the sword, for you have insufficient skill in warfare, or if you have learned to wage war, you make yourself ready for worldly business more than for Christ's business, you practise forensic law more than ecclesiastical law, you are more clever in worldly combat than in combat of the spirit.

Heb 4:12

Sg 3:8

The Prince of the Church wants a man of the

Church who is ready, wants him ready to give account of the faith and the hope which is in us.* If you are lethargic and inexpert in these virtues, on what score can you boast that you have a ready answer for questions of public law? In the mouth of a cleric or of a monk sacred literature sounds much more fitting than secular. Why do you wish to speak Egyptian in Jerusalem?⁶ That is not what Isaiah says: 'There will be five cities in the land of Egypt which speak the language of Canaan,'* that is to say, because quite unversed in Hebrew, they might speak the language nearest to Hebrew; because they could not speak the holy tongue, they might speak one closely related to the holy tongue. Why seek 'to speak half in the language of Ashdod, when you ought to speak the language of Judah'? So indeed, we read in Esdras.* Speak the tongues not of men but of Angels.† You are indeed an angel of God, since you profess the ministry of the sacred word. 'For the lips of a priest guard knowledge and men will demand the law from his mouth, for he is a messenger of the Lord of hosts.'*

1 P 3:15; G. adds: [fide et] spe, as in S 26:8.

Is 19:18

2 Ezra (Nehemiah) 13:24

†1 Co 13:1

Ml 2:7

5. ·Since you are a man of the Gospel, let yours be wholly the language of the Gospel. Let your speech then smack of the Law, the prophets, the apostles; sharpen your tongue on their words; borrow from them weapons wielded for God to demolish fortresses and to topple every sophistry exalting itself above the knowledge of God.* Let 'the sword of the spirit' be 'versatile' in your grasp,* a trusty servant for every task confronting you. Let your skill in the sacred word not fail you, when the need of the moment suddenly requires it. Let the word of power and might be on your lips not in your notes, for 'the lips of a priest' not his notes 'should guard knowledge'.* Take this 'purse full of money' with you:*⁷ let the sword of the word be at your side, not in hiding; let it be the thing closest to yourself. Gird it upon your thigh, that you may be powerful and prompt both 'to encourage with sound doctrine' and to refute adversaries.*⁸ Let your sword not be beneath your thigh and do not subordinate the

2 Co 10:5
Eph 6:17; Gn 3:24

Ml 2:7
Pr 7:20

Tt 1:9

study of the sacred word to prudence of the flesh.

'Each with his sword at his thigh:'* to one teacher is granted the lesson of knowledge, to another the lesson of wisdom, and to each his own grace from the spirit.* 'Each with his sword at his thigh', so that where the chance of assault exists, there may be a greater recourse to the word and more frequent warnings. 'Each one with his sword at his thigh', in order that he may be the first to correct himself, to safeguard himself, to put himself on trial.* Paul teaches you to have your sword at your thigh when he says: 'Take heed for yourself, lest you also be tempted.'* 'Each one with his sword at his thigh, against alarms by night', against sudden lapses, unexpected falls.

The apostle implies a kind of nocturnal alarm when he says: 'If any man is caught off guard in some wrongdoing.'* For 'nocturnal' means what is unexpected and sudden; 'nocturnal' also means what is insidious. So Paul warns: 'lest we be outwitted by Satan; for we are not unaware of his wiles.'* In another verse the same Paul was afraid of a nocturnal alarm: 'I am afraid', he says, 'that as the serpent seduced Eve, so your ideas may be led astray from the simplicity which is in Christ.'* Good is that simplicity, where you who 'cling to Christ are one spirit with him'.*[9] Simplicity exists where unity exists. Simplicity exists, if you live no longer, but Christ lives in you,* if the wisdom of God consumes you, if spiritual joy absorbs you and seeps into your inmost marrow. And where is such simplicity save in his little bed?

6. 'Each with his sword at his thigh.' 'At his thigh', not against the thigh but 'against alarms by night', perhaps because their struggle is not 'against flesh and blood' denoted by the thigh but 'against the world rulers of this darkness'. And so 'against alarms by night' means against hosts of evil spirits.[10] How much happier a struggle fell to your lot, for you are carried in Solomon's bed! You struggle not against carnal or even against spiritual wickedness, but with spiritual gladness, with Solomon who has first claim

Sg 3:8

1 Co 12:7-10

2 Tm 3:16; 1 Tm 5:22; 1 Co 14:29

Ga 6:1

Ga 6:1

2 Co 2:11

2 Co 11:3

1 Co 6:17

Ga 2:20

to the name of 'Peacemaker'. Therefore your wrestling with him is the making of peace. Solomon not only bears the name of Peacemaker but also personifies Wisdom.

'Love Wisdom' he says, 'and she will embrace you.'[11] An embrace bears some resemblance to a struggle. Embrace her ·that she may embrace you. 'You will be honored by her, when you have embraced her', as Solomon says in Proverbs.* Embrace the Word, treat the Word as if you were in his little bed not as if in a duel. His little bed is no place for drawn swords but for close embraces. Do not arm yourself as a guard, lest you find yourself on guard outside. Snug inside, reach for the Word, not as a sword but as a spouse, that you may be embraced by the Word personally.[12] May you be embraced by Truth in Person, and not wrestle against errors and vices; leave this task and duty to others. What business have you with wrangling, whose whole concern ought to be with affections? One who is a bride does not seek the task of argument and refutation but rather the freedom to embrace.[13] Let others take their places around his little bed; it is yours to enjoy his long-desired embraces.

Pr 4:8

7. Why are we told nothing about the furnishings of his little bed, nothing to suggest an inkling of its delights? Perhaps this word is an ineffable word and not licit for a human to utter. One who experiences this word understands it, but only momentarily while the experience lasts, and not even from memory can one fully recall past delights. Scripture expressed what it could. It mentioned a little bed and Solomon's little bed. One word is enough, but only for the wise!* I read both of Solomon's throne and of his carriage, but of both as displaying courtly trappings in keeping with a king's luxury.* Are we then to deduce that the little bed is neglected? Far from it; but it was enough for the writer who was addressing the bride to refer to his 'little bed'. For she will cherish nothing in the little bed but the fact that it is his little bed and that it

Plautus, The Persian, *2:4:15*

1 K 10:18-20. See Miquel, pp. 155-6.

provided the freedom to embrace her own Solomon.

You will find a wealth of hidden meanings in the little beds throughout the text of Scripture, but there is none to compare with the little bed of Solomon. There is the bed which Job spreads for himself in darkness and the bed which David waters with his tears.* There is the bed on which the sick man lies and the bed from which the dead child rises.* Such was the bed of Elisha; such was that of Elijah. Each raised the dead son of their hostess from his little bed.* Elisha stretched himself over the dead boy; Elijah bowed over him. The one Christ is in each of them. 'He emptied himself to take the form of a servant',* and compressed the length of his eternity into the shortness of a nature subject to time. He expanded himself, when he bountifully poured his holy Spirit into us. That mother's bosom could hug her dead boy but could not restore his life. 'For the letter kills, the Spirit gives life.'* But the true Elijah carried the boy to his upper room and drew him to an understanding of the spirit. Cold was the bosom of the letter and its understanding was unable to breathe vital warmth. Good was the bed of Elijah for he poured the warmth of life into the dead boy. 'The just man lives by faith.'* That is why Elijah measured himself over the dead boy three times, that he might confer a knowledge of the Trinity and 'apportion the measure of faith'.*

The Law mourns over the dead sense of the letter,[14] the carnal sense, but Christ withdrew this sense and restored the spiritual sense. He restored to the letter a new and vital meaning which he might recognize as truly his own, for he is the Elijah who restored and made all things new.* Paul also says that he is dead to the Law that he may live in Christ.* It is good that you too should die not only to the old Law but also to the old self, that he may give you life in his bed, who bore our sins in his body in order that 'dead to sin, we might live in righteousness'.* For 'what you sow is not given new life unless it first dies'.* We are all understood in the risen Christ and therefore his Resurrection is a grace common to all.*

But in the little bed of Solomon there is some particular grace reserved as a privilege for the bride alone.

8. Even now, good Jesus, if a son of our mother be dead—I mean a son of this holy community,[15] this widow with whom (so to speak) you lodge—do you restore him to life. That son is dead who is crushed by the weight either of tedium or of despair, who possesses no lively devotion, no fervor of spirit, who although he does not abandon the precepts of the Law and hides himself in the lap of the Rule, none the less languishes in a cold and moribund affection and feels no sweetness in our holy work. The sorrowful countenance of the whole Order disheartens him. He must be cherished in the soft and womanly bosom of his mother, that he may not become rebellious and 'be broken by excessive sorrow'.* He should not be found outside the embrace of his mother's bosom, lest perhaps the true[16] Elijah should fail to take him to his upper room. Consider those whom Christ raises to life; everywhere he grants this gift, thanks to the tears of women. So he raised the widow's son* and the brother of the holy women;* so at the prayers of her parents he raised their daughter.*

2 Co 2:7

Lk 7:12-15
Jn 11:11-44
Lk 8:49-55

Raise also this dead brother of ours, good Jesus, from his mother's bosom. This outward observance of our Rule leads no one to perfection.* Lead him to the softer bed of a better hope, by which he may draw near to God. Let him experience what he is awaiting, 'for good is the Lord' to those who wait for him, 'to the soul which seeks him'.* This experience of an hour brings gladness to the labors of many seasons.* Then is restored to his mother the son she had lost before, while she did not retain his affection but wept over his dead devotion. He returns to us renewed, after you have clothed him with yourself. You stretch yourself over him like this that you may cover what is repulsive and clothe what is naked. Good is the use of this little bed, which in a brief hour injects a lively eagerness for the seasons to come. There is greater grace in the little bed of Solomon, for in it the bride, leaving her mother according

See Lam 195,
n. 167; 170, n. 5

Lm 3:25

See Miquel,
p. 156, n. 21.

to the flesh, clings to her Beloved in an everlasting bond and becomes one spirit with him.* [1 Co 6:17]

9. Good then is the little bed in which there is no languor except perhaps the languor of love, for it is not concerned with weakness but with rejoicing. Good is the little bed which is not watered by tears, not spread in darkness, which has in it nothing sorrowful, nothing dark, but is wholly light and gladness, which need not be spread with brocaded coverlets from Egypt with which the heretical woman in Proverbs spreads her little bed.* [Pr 7:16] For the little bed of Solomon has in it no imported ornament, no gaudy painting, no worldly pomp; it is nothing but holy pleasure and sound truth. Great and varied is the meaning hidden in the little beds of holy men, but the little bed of Solomon surpasses them all.[17] Even the bride's little bed cannot stand comparison with Solomon's. In her little bed she does not find the Beloved whom she is seeking, so she rises and makes her rounds until she reaches him. Hasten, daughter, hasten, consecrated virgin, hasten to enter into his retreat. Have no fear of the drawn swords surrounding it. Those swords, swords of the word, against the thigh and against alarms by night, either transfix the wantonness of the flesh or excise the cowardice of a timid heart. This they do in others, but you they wound more gently, that transfixed by perfect love you may know nothing of alarms by night and may have no blend of chilling fear, but may pass wholly into the affection of burning love, for you have been consecrated to the undivided practice of love and destined to ascend to the place[18] of perfect love, the couch of your Beloved, the little bed of the true Solomon, Jesus Christ, who lives and reigns for ever and ever. Amen.* [See Lam 14, n. 53]

NOTES ON SERMON SIXTEEN

1. Although G. addresses one person throughout S 16, from S 17 one sees that this sermon was intended for nuns literally or as a literary device. Mikkers, p. 38, suggests that S 16, 17, 18, and perhaps 40 and 45:6 were intended for nuns. One might argue that S 15-21, where G. discusses a choral unit in the Canticle, Sg 3:6-11, was used by him in a series of talks to nuns; see 'Nuns in the Audience of Gilbert of Hoyland' in a forthcoming volume of the subseries Medieval Cistercian History (Kalamazoo Cistercian Studies Conference). On the little bed, *lectulus*, see Lam 21, n. 92.

2. Ps 71:7; 'until the moon is no more', *donec auferatur luna*, in Mab. but omitted by Migne; it is needed for what follows.

3. On S 16: 1, 2, 5, 9, see M.-André Fracheboud, 'Divinisation' DSp 3 (1957) 1407-8; Gilson, *Mystical Theology*, p. 229, n. 75, and *History of Christian Philosophy in the Middle Ages* (N.Y.: Randon House, 1954) p. 633, n. 110.

4. Flor. and Migne may be right to omit the bracketed clause in this sentence of Mab. *Pretium eius est propter quod ipse se impendit, [quod ipse se impendit,] quod ipse se aestimat, quo eius expletur aviditas.*

5. Reading *pagina*, rather than *vagina* with Mab. and Migne; *pagina* is the reading in several mss. e.g. Paris 9605, Troyes 410, and has G's humorous touch.

6. *lingua aegyptia*. On secular learning, see G. E2:2; Lam 177, n. 46.

7. Mab., Flor., mss. Paris 9605, Troyes 419: *Sacculum pecuniae tolle tecum*, omitted by Migne.

8. Roger Sherman Loomis, 'The Grail, from Celtic Myth to Christian Symbol', (N.Y., Columbia U.P., 1963) p. 189, in showing the influence of G. on the *Queste del Saint Graal*, quotes three of the last four sentences and continues: 'Thus the symbolism of the sword was fixed by St Paul, and the obligation of the Christian to hang it by his side was proclaimed by Abbot Gilbert.' See Bouton, 'Fiches Cisterciennes', pp. 225-8.

9. Mab. and ms. Troyes 410: *es*; Migne and ms. Paris 9605: *est*.

10. G. *contra spirituales nequitias*; Vulg. *contra spiritualia nequitiae*.

11. G. *Ama sapientiam et amplexabitur te*; Vulg. *Dilige eam et conservabit te*.

12. G. plays on *oblecteris* and *oblucteris* to the confusion of editors.

13. See Leclercq, 'Otia Monastica', 121:33.

14. De Lubac, *Exégèse*, II:142, n. 6, on *sensum exstinctum litterae*.

15. *Conventus hujus sancti*, see Lam 13, n. 46, 19, n. 79.

16. Reading *verus* with Migne, rather than *vetus* with Mab.

17. Mab: *supergressus est universos lectulus Salamonis, nec*, omitted in Migne.

18. Mab: *locum*; Migne: *lacum*.

SERMON 17
THE RICH CARRIAGE

The bride is carried in a rich carriage on her way to her Solomon. 1. Solomon's carriage is spiritual for it is inlaid with charity. 2. Everyone should be a carriage for Christ, but not everyone a preacher of the word. 3. Why be vainglorious when you received from another all you have? 4. Seek the good reputation of a clear conscience, the good odor of Paul's sanctity. 5. Virginal purity, especially that of Mary, is suggested by the wood of Lebanon. 6. Vices make pure balsam rank; Satan is a compounder of counterfeit balsam. 7–8. Learn from the Scriptures and the Doctors the right proportions for your perfume.

SOLOMON MADE HIMSELF A CARRIAGE FROM THE WOOD OF LEBANON, HE MADE ITS POSTS OF SILVER, ITS COUCH OF GOLD*[1] *Sg 3:9*

You heard, holy virgins, brides of Christ, you heard in yesterday's sermon about the little bed of your Solomon. In today's sermon hasten to inquire further about the hidden meaning of his carriage. You wish to direct all interpretations of this Canticle to the exercise of love and to apply them for your delight. You think these songs were written for you alone. No words have any bouquet of wisdom for you unless they blossom with affections of love and emit the sweet fragrance of charity. So here also you have a verse which suggests the endearments of love; the divine word refers you to his carriage. Your Beloved does not allow you any pretext for sitting idle. Pleasant indeed are the promised joys of his little bed, but possibly some anxiety about the difficulty of reaching them might still be whispered among you. So this text describes for you in its fair variety the furnishings of the sacred coach, in which you are to be carried to his little bed. Even on your journey your Bridegroom himself provides you with delights.

This carriage is pleasing indeed in its material but more pleasing in its maker. For Solomon is both designer and craftsman for this carriage. 'King Solomon made himself a carriage from the wood of Lebanon. He made its posts of silver, its couch of gold.' Hear, daughter, in what a splendid equipage you are carried to his bed. The Bridegroom does not leave you without a couch, one of gold, perhaps of that gold of which you read that 'his head is the purest gold'.* The couch has many uses, but all less exalted than those of the little bed. On a couch weary hope has a comfortable support but in a bed hope yields to enjoyment. In the former the bride's desire is encouraged, in the latter she enjoys its fruition. What luxury awaits you, do you think, when you are conveyed in such splendor? Why should I now with many a reference make a complete inventory: the cedar wood, the wood of Lebanon, the silver posts? The material beauty ringing in our ears appeals to us and its beauty applied figuratively tends to suggest some splendor of the spirit and of the understanding and to indicate a couch for a holy soul. The context of the passage does not allow these words to be understood in a material sense, for why would the gold metal be inlaid with charity? No, every detail is spiritual, because spiritual is that love to which you are invited by a carriage furnished so elegantly.

Sg 5:11

Sermon Seventeen

2. I could apply these and similar features of his carriage according to our interpretation. Let it be enough to have dealt with them briefly either to satisfy or to arouse your eagerness. What? Do you wish these songs to serve you alone? Let the young girls be fed, let them turn some few verses to their own advantage. Christ is a debtor to the wise and to the simple.* He is no way poorer for you, if he is richer for others in his own sense.* Be content with the little bed; allow the use even of his carriage to assist the younger generation. The grace of his little bed is rarer, that of the carriage is more common. In the former Christ is at rest; in the latter he is on the way. He grants himself to you more abundantly and with special privileges, yet he does not forget other maidens, even though they cannot yet reach your stature.

Rm 1:14
Rm 14:5. See Bouton, "Fiches Cistérciennes", p. 239.

You also can share the mystery of the carriage and play the role of carriages, if you carry down to us, as it were, the Bridegroom whom you hold in cloister, if you bring peace, if you announce good tidings, if you proclaim outwardly the joys which you see within.* Were they not carriages from whose Office we chant in the Church: 'carrying peace and enlightening their fatherland?'² But let no one assume the office of preaching, 'let no one take the honor to himself'* unless he is called by God. Why set yourself up on a candlestick, when you do not enlighten yourself? Let him set you on high who made you a lamp. Ascend through him who lights your lamp.

Is 52:7. See Lam 18, n. 78; 17, n. 68.

Heb 5:4

According to our text, no one makes himself a carriage, but Solomon personally made a carriage for himself from the wood of Lebanon. Yet that person is also a carriage who carries Christ not only on the lips but also in the body. 'Glorify and carry Christ in your body',* says Paul. Paul wishes Christ to be carried by you, but proudly, not with tedium, not with complaint, not with indignation and a wavering resolution. Paul wants Him carried, not dragged. For to anyone who drags him, Christ is burdensome: chastity is a burden, humiliation is a burden, obedience is an onus, poverty is squalid. You are a

1 Co 6:20

misshapen porter, if such is your deportment! Faith seems to you a heavy rod and piety cumbersome. You cannot say: 'My Beloved is a sachet of myrrh for me.'* So your faith seems to you like a cart-load of hay, for under its weight you creak and groan and complain 'as a wagon creaks when loaded with hay'.* Christ is not a load of hay but a flower and a fruit and the tree of life, a tree which gives fruit in due season*³ and are you unwilling to wait? Blessed are they who eat in due season.* Patience says Paul, is needed if you are to reap the promises.* Then carry your burdens in patience, yes, the burdens of piety. For piety itself also has a part in the promise, as Paul writes to Timothy.*

^{margin:} Sg 1:12; Rm 11:20; Qo 24:17; Sg 5:15
Am 2:13
Gn 2:9; Ps 1:3.
Qo 10:17
Heb 10:36; Lam 198, n. 185.
1 Tm 4:8

3. Then carry the image of him who is from heaven and carry his image proudly, for his burden is light.* Be not an ignominious stumbling-block but a proud coach such as King Solomon made for himself. Surprisingly, however, Paul carefully distinguishes the various virtues, so as first to exclude the hollowness of boasting. 'For what have you that you did not receive? If then you received it, why do you boast as if it were not a gift?'* If you are a carriage, you did not make yourself but he made you. For 'King Solomon made himself a carriage from the wood of Lebanon'. And who made the very wood? Did he not? He planted the cedars of Lebanon. But if you are a lofty cedar of Lebanon, 'do not have lofty thoughts but be fearful' lest perhaps in your elation you be uprooted from the place where you were planted by election.* For you did not elect yourself but he elected you for the work of the ministry.* He confers the office of the ministry, he confers the grace to minister, that is, both the power and the honor. Recognize by whom you were planted and let not the root of pride approach you, so that the hand of the tempter may not stir you. Let no axe of the enemy be raised to cut you down; for not even his razor is raised over the head of the saints.* He dances for joy at whisking off for himself any carriage of God and at felling trees of Lebanon for his own designs. In Ezechiel he brays his brag: 'I have sat on the throne

^{margin:} Mt 11:30
1 Co 4:7
Rm 11:20; Qo 24:17; Sg 5:15
Eph 4:12
1 S 1:11

of God.'* Take care lest through elation you be transformed from a throne of righteousness into a throne of pestilence* and a carriage of scandal. Take care lest through you either bad example or evil gossip 'spread like a plague'* to the ruin of many. Be a carriage of God, that you may carry his image in yourself and that through you 'he may spread the fragrance of his acquaintance'.* Such a carriage was Paul, of whom the Lord himself proclaims: 'He is a chosen instrument of mine to carry my name.'* He elected Paul. He made him his carriage.

Ezk 38:2

Ps 1:1

2 Tm 2:17

2 Co 2:14

Ac 9:15

4. 'King Solomon made himself a carriage from the wood of Lebanon.' This is cedarwood and by its own nature and by the name of its place of origin, it portends something great. Lebanon means purity, for its wood is impervious to corruption; as its substance does not admit decay, so it emits a most delicate fragrance. Truly Paul was of Lebanon, for he served God, as he himself says, 'with a clear conscience'.* For what is purer than a clear conscience? What is less subject to decay than one whom no creature could separate from the love of God?* Virtues of a moment which serve their brief hour, seem to me not so much wood as plants which quickly perish.* But in Paul was the incorruptibility of unflagging charity. So he 'fought the good fight, finished the race', thenceforth looking for 'the crown of righteousness',* a crown of sheaves whose fragrance, close by, he already inhaled. Then, as he says, he breathed forth a goodly fragrance, 'fragrance from life to life', the 'fragrance of the knowledge of God'.* A good fragrance is a good reputation; a good fragrance is also a good conscience. The former breathes its bouquet for others, the latter for itself. Indeed the glory of the saints is the witness of their conscience.* The fruits of future beatitude have already begun to breathe their bouquet for us in goodness of life. A good fragrance is rightly added to freedom from corruption, but contrariwise decay has a rank odor. The man who sows in the flesh will reap from the flesh corruption* and from corruption a putrid odor, just

2 Tm 1:3

Rm 8:39

Ps 36:2

2 Tm 4:7

2 Co 2:14-15

2 Co 1:2

Ga 6:8

as from integrity breathes a sweet fragrance.

5. Rightly integrity has been mentioned, because virginal purity seems to be indicated by the wood of Lebanon. Virginal continence also emits a good fragrance and it is enjoyed for ever. Whether or not the yoke of marriage will be abolished or the desolation of widows be ended, yet the freedom and grace of virginal integrity will never pass away,* for those who neither marry nor are given in marriage are already like the angels in heaven.* Again in Scripture virginity is compared to Lebanon: 'Like uncut frankincense of Lebanon I turned into perfume and like pure balsam was my fragrance.'* Deservedly described as Lebanon is the immaculate womb, the womb undefiled, untouched and uncut. Uncut is the womb whose integrity remains, the enclosure of whose chastity has not been unsealed. Such a womb is a Lebanon through purity and uncut through integrity. Rightly is she called uncut, who is not divided. Would you hear of one who is cut? 'The married woman is anxious about the affairs of the world, how to please her husband, and so she is divided', divided indeed between God and her husband, and perhaps not equally divided but more inclined towards her husband. 'But the unmarried woman or the virgin thinks only about the affairs of the Lord',* how to please God.

'Like uncut frankincense of Lebanon, I filled my dwellingplace with fragrance.'* These words seem to belong especially to the Mother of the Lord. She was really the frankincense of Lebanon and Lebanon uncut. She filled her dwelling-place with fragrance, holy virgins, a heavenly dwelling-place, an angelic dwelling-place, when she filled you with examples of a virginal way of life and inspired you with the love of perpetual chastity. And she expressed quite clearly the grace of her dwelling-place, which she says was filled with fragrance. For what is more like perfume than a virginal dwelling-place? This way of life has nothing carnal about it, nothing worldly, but all is heavenly, otherworldly,[4] spiritual, and therefore like perfume. But what kind of perfume? 'And my

See 1 Co 13:8

Mt 22:30

Si 24:21

1 Co 7:34

Qo 24:21

fragrance,' says the text, 'is like pure balsam.' Like balsam that is pure, not rank, not adulterated. There is a mixture which simulates balsam and is counterfeit; and there is a mixture which although possessing no similarity to balsam makes perfume rank. There is then, to enumerate: balsam which is genuine and unadulterated; balsam which although genuine is adulterated; balsam which is neither genuine nor unadulterated. The first is found in the perfect, the last in those who are deceived; the central balsam in those who although not deluded by any fallacy, lack the grace of some virtue. Rightly then does she who alone was full of grace say that her 'fragrance was like pure balsam'.

6. Now if yours is the fragrance of virginity, of persistent prayer, of fast and abstinence, yours is a good fragrance, the fragrance of balsam. But if you still suffer from the malady of impatience, if gossip, fickle resolution, determination to do your own will, moroseness, tedium—if any of these is reported in you, your perfume is still mixed and you do not breathe forth the fragrance of pure balsam.* For a slight drop of some foreign element spoils the whole essence of balsam. It is well with the person who immediately brushes aside any drop of sadness which may appear by chance or on a sudden. 'For in many ways we all offend', says James.* From a sudden fall, immediately corrected, no odor is noticeable; malodor comes rather from a vice in which one persists.

See Lam 1 76, n. 38

Jm 3:2

Perilous and poisonous is the mixture when some vice is disguised as a virtue; even an angel of Satan 'appears as an angel of light',* and, as it were, makes poison smell like balsam. Satan is a compounder of perfumes; buy no oil from him. Indeed he is not so much a compounder as a confounder of ointments! Consider Job's words: 'He makes the sea bubble like a cauldron; he churns the sea like ointment brought to a boil.'* Death is in his cauldron.† This cauldron Jeremiah saw boiling, its contents tilting from the north.* What sort of perfumer is he who pretends that from the cauldron of death issue the vapors of

2 Co 11:14

Jb 41:31
†*2 K 4:40*

Jr 1:13

life? What sort of perfumer is he who pretends that the spout of a boiling cauldron pours steam from the south, when through its spout evils are kindled upon earth rather from the north? Either the son of a prophet or surely a prophet himself has discerned that death is in the cauldron and that its steam comes from the north. Sulfurous is the steam which the boiling cauldron of your flesh emits and do you imagine you smell in it the fragrance of balsam?

If you haven't the skill yourself to discern genuine from counterfeit balsam, come to the prophets, come to the sons of prophets, the apostles, who teach you the different kinds of mixtures and in which cauldron death hides. Such is Paul, who dared to say: 'We are not ignorant of his wiles.'* If your own hand is unable to procure genuine balsam for you, let the saints teach you how to mix it. Nicodemus brought a mixture of myrrh and aloes about a hundred weight and the Marys bought ointments.* But Mary the Mother of the Lord does not so much procure as breathe forth ointments, for she gave birth to Christ himself who is anointed with the oil of gladness.* 'Like pure balsam,' says the text, 'is my fragrance.'

7. If you are ignorant of the proportions in the mixture, come to the doctors of the Church, to those who are like the pillars and the foundation of truth,* the silver posts of the Lord's carriage and dispensers of the holy word;* learn from them how to think of the affairs of the Lord and how to be 'concerned for Christ that you may please him'.* Then you also will have silver posts in yourself, if you are supported by knowledge of both Testaments. That is why here, after the wood of Lebanon, the inspired text refers to the silver posts, that you may hold 'the mystery of faith in a pure conscience'.* 'The mystery of faith' which the sacred text sets before you is a text of silver, in order that relying on the precepts of the Gospels and of the apostles you may meditate on them, cherish them, and compare them in your heart. May you not allow the silver of the divine word to be shut tight on some dusty shelf, there to become

blurred and tarnished with the patina of neglect.

8. But we cannot now insert these pillars into today's sermon. The logs of Lebanon preempted the space in this tract and, allured by their perfume, our sermon followed their fragrance further than I intended. *To you, Lord, I commend this Lebanon, this noble Lebanon, this choir of virgins, this assembly of consecrated women. Guard it, that it may not be cut down and may remain uncut. Let integrity be reserved for it and the purity of its chastity, for Lebanon means purity. Let purity of intention be preserved that all may be holy in body and spirit. Safeguard this Lebanon, for you have consecrated its wood as material for your carriage. Far from this Lebanon be the threat of the prophet: 'Open your gates, O Lebanon; let fire devour your cedars.'* Let these gates be barred to others but open to you. Be their key and their enclosure;* seal and unseal,† that they may welcome neither seal nor key other than you, Christ Jesus, who are God blessed for ever and ever. Amen.*

Zc 11:1
*Rv 3:7
†Rv 5:9

NOTES ON SERMON SEVENTEEN

1. G. refers to this sermon as a *tractatus* in par. 8, and in large part he addresses one individual. His references to 'the little bed', to 'Solomon as Peacemaker' and to the 'good tidings' confirm his statement that he used S 16 the day before to the same audience of nuns, but wishes now to include advice for the young girls present. His adaptations are evident in the first half of par. 1, and 2, in the transition to 3, in one sentence of 5, and in the final paragraph. See Jean Leclercq, 'La première rédaction des *Sermones in Cantica* de Gilbert de Hoyland', R Ben. 62 (1952) 289-90.
2. 'In the Office for apostles', Mab. For other liturgical texts in G, see S 32:7, 33:8, 40:4 and 6.
3. Reading *lignum* with Migne, mss. Paris 9605 and Troyes 419, rather than *signum* with Mab.
4. For *supermundanum*, see M.-A. Fracheboud, 'Denys l'Aréopagite: en Occident, 3. Les Cistérciens', DSp 329-39; in c. 336, the author lists the following compounds: *supereminens laetitia*, S 12:3, 62D; *supereminere sapientia*, S 5:8, 36C; *supereminere angelis*, S 7:6, 46A; *supermundanum*, S 17:5, 90B; *superpulchra*, S 29:1 150A. Ms. Paris 6905: *supermundanum;* Troyes 419: *super mundanum*.

SERMON 18
PURIFICATION, BELIEF, VISION,
IMITATION

The bride is purified, believes, beholds, and imitates. 1. The silver pillars are knowledge of the faith and meditation on the Scriptures. 2. Vices turn the silver tongue of a virgin to lead. 3. Silver pillars mean an orderly knowledge of the faith, and the golden couch the vision of truth in rapture. 4. How Lebanon, the silver pillars, and the golden couch are steps leading to contemplation, here a fleeting glimpse from the rays of his Light. 5. One on whom He sheds a ray of his light, changes from night into day; the head of divine Majesty nowhere reclines more readily than on the golden couch of virginity. 6. Humility is won by following the purple steps of the royal Christ.

KING SOLOMON MADE HIMSELF A CARRIAGE FROM THE WOOD OF LEBANON. HE MADE ITS PILLARS OF SILVER, ITS COUCH OF GOLD, ITS STEPS OF PURPLE*[1] Sg 3:9

I n the wood of Lebanon was expressed for you freedom from corruption in the flesh and the splendor of purity. Good indeed is chastity but 'what is not from faith is sin'.* 'By faith', says Rm 14:23
Peter, 'God purified the hearts of the Gentiles.'* Ac 15:9
For chastity is not judged by bodily continence alone; it is esteemed much more for purity of heart. 'You are already made clean', says Jesus, 'by the word which I have spoken to you.'* Good is the Jn 15:3

word of faith which cleanses, and so in building his carriage he inserts, after the wood of Lebanon, the silver pillars and summons the mind of virginal purity to meditation on the sacred word, the chaste word, the word which is compared to chastened silver.* Good are pillars anchored in the breast of virgins, if they are supported by faithful knowledge and frequent consideration of sacred Scripture. You are a good Lebanon, if you have a clean heart, cleansed of impure thoughts and thoughts of unbelief.

A great defilement of the spirit is the decay of faith. If, however, a strong formation in faith remains vigorous in you, you already hold one pillar. Do not be content with this; add a second pillar: meditate 'on the law of the Lord day and night'.* Regard it as infidelity and fornication if your mind turns away in the least from reflection on the faith. Good pillars are the knowledge and remembrance of the divine law and an upright belief in and mindfulness of the faith. You are a pillar if you are steadfast in faith. You are a pillar of silver if you have been schooled in the use of the divine word. 'Upright is the work of the Lord', says the Psalmist, 'and all his works are trustworthy.'* Good pillars are faith and the word of faith. Let this word be ready in your heart, for it is ready on your lips; let it be ready and ever present in your heart. From the abundance of the heart, words flow upon the lips.* 'Seven times a day,' says the prophet, 'I have sung your praises.'* You holy virgins, always sing his praises. Seven times, of course, sing his praise according to the canonical hours, at all times singing and chanting in your hearts.*

2. Let your tongues be of silver. They are of silver, if they ring out Christ from the sacred page. Let no lump of lead be put into your mouth. The mouth is of lead which utters nothing refined, nothing sharp, nothing from above, but is wholly slack, wholly blunt, wholly from below, perhaps even from the wicked. For wickedness sits in the talent of lead.* Not of lead were the talents which the man in the Gospel distributed to his servants when he went

Sermon Eighteen

abroad on a journey.* Do not trade with talents of lead; let none of them be found in your treasure chests. Listen to Paul's advice: 'Let no evil talk come out of your mouth but only what is good for building the faith.'* 'For building,' he says, not for toppling the faith. A mouth of iron topples the faith, undermines holy conversation, is an engine of war, a seedbed of strife, for it rings out complaint and bitterness.* Such a beast is described in Daniel, with iron teeth and claws, munching and crunching all things.* Let no such beast be found among the little sheep² or rather among the friends of the Lord.*

In this virginal flock let there be no venomous, no violent beast; in this paradise let no serpent's hiss be heard.* Venomous words do not befit a virgin's lips. Individually, what are you doing? With your lips defiled with foul words, will you plant a kiss on the lips of your Beloved? He is 'the purity of eternal light' and 'nothing defiled' comes into contact with him.* Remember that your lips are dedicated to heavenly kisses and prophecies. Consider it sacrilege if your lips utter anything not sweet, not divine, not from the sacred page. 'Blow the trumpet at the new moon', says the Psalm, 'on the special day of your solemnity.'* For you every day should be solemn, always a new moon, always a sabbath. Therefore let your lips be like a trumpet of beaten silver;* a trumpet which summons not to strife but to gladness, celebration, spiritual canticles.

3. I do not know how our talk veered from silver pillars to trumpets, except that one whose lips are a silver trumpet is a sterling pillar in the house of the Lord. A good pillar is one upon whom the weary are supported. You can consult Isaiah: 'The Lord has given me a learned tongue, that I may know how to support with a word one who has slipped.'* The tongue of Christ Jesus was obviously learned as he proclaimed peace and preached goodness. 'A gentle tongue is a tree of life',* 'a pillar and prop of truth.'* Do you also, O virgin, carry the image of your Bridegroom for this purpose, that you may have a learned tongue, a gentle tongue, not erroneous,

Mt 25:14-15

Ep 4:29

Lam 17, n. 70
Dn 7:7

amicas Domini.
See *Lam 17, n. 69*

See *Lam 19, n. 83*

Ws 7:26, 25

Ps 80:4. See Leclercq, 'Otia Monastica,' 91:37; *Lam 10, n. 33*
Nb 10:2

Is 50:4

Pr 15:4
1 Tm 3:15

not rambling, not gossipy, but a tongue which speaks judiciously, proffers a word of comfort, a tongue which is a pillar and prop 'for building the faith', whether your own or that of another. Let 'the word of faith' be 'ready on your lips and in your heart'.*

Would you hear about the silver pillar? 'The law of his God is in his heart'—there is the silver; 'and his steps will not slip'*—there is the pillar. Rightly is one a pillar, who cannot be toppled. 'By the word of the Lord the heavens were made firm',* says the psalmist. By this word let the heart of a virgin be made firm, that it may be a heaven, a throne of God, and become a couch of gold. In silver, understand an orderly knowledge of the faith; in gold, the brilliance of understanding and truth. This golden couch is set on posts of silver, for 'unless you have believed, you will not understand'.* Instruction in the faith provides a step towards purity of understanding. On this foundation rests the grace of contemplation. While you meditate with faith on the word of God and by patience and the consolation of Scripture raise yourself up to celestial hope, you show that you are a pillar. Then you rise as a golden couch, when naked truth without the cloak of speech, begins to flash upon you in rapture.*

4. Now review more carefully the orderly progress from the wood of Lebanon to the silver pillars and the golden couch. Clearly in Lebanon shines purity of heart; in silver shines knowledge of God's Law; in gold or the ministry of the word shine the sacred mysteries. In Lebanon you cleanse the eye of your mind, in silver you observe, but in gold you perceive; or if you prefer, you are purified, you meditate and you contemplate. 'Praise and beauty', the psalmist says, 'are in his sight'.* In Lebanon beauty is proposed to you, in silver praise, in gold the sight of the divine Presence. How great is the grace of this praise and beauty, since it is welcome in the sight of such Majesty! Would you hear of this distinction in another psalm? 'A clean heart create in me, O God, and an upright spirit renew within me. Cast me not

Rm 10:8

Ps 36:31

Ps 32:6

Is 7:9 (LXX)

Lam 182, n. 77

Ps 95:6; Lam 183, n. 77

from your face.'* You see how 'deep calls to deep',† how different passages of Scripture chant in harmony. Refer the first words to the purity of Lebanon: 'For blessed are the clean of heart, because they shall see God.'* Refer the second to the pillars of silver: 'For the word of the Lord is upright.'* Refer the third to the golden couch, where the face of the Lord is clearly seen without any veil, and in the gold gleams his royal Majesty; that is to say, the psalmist asks for the gift of a purified, an instructed and, so to speak, a dazzled spirit. In Lebanon he is purified, in silver he is instructed, in gold he is dazzled. For the vision of any purified mind is indeed dazzled in contemplation and can sustain for only a moment the flashes of inner enlightenment.

*Ps 50:12-13
†Ps 41:8; de Lubac, Exégèse, 1:349, n. 3
Mt 5:8
Ps 32:4

In your turn retrace these stages of progress, if you aspire to the grace of contemplation. Let nothing defiled, let no element of unbelief remain in you, that the naked truth can flash upon you. First be cleansed, secondly be trained, thirdly be contemplative. Be cleansed from the law of the flesh, be trained in the law of faith, watch and behold in the law of perfect freedom, in the law of the Spirit. For 'where the Spirit of the Lord is, there is freedom',* in that law which is free from the veil of the letter, in which there is place neither for error nor ignorance nor riddles. Where error exists, it leads astray; where ignorance exists, it fails to lead; where riddles exist though they lead, they do not lead all the way. But there who would go astray? For there is the couch, and repose, and the end of longings. Who would remain in ignorance? For the couch is of gold and it gleams in the light. What riddle is there? The end of longings and the calm of truth leave no place for the figurative language of riddles. There is nothing counterfeit, nothing hidden, nothing figurative. There is gold and it gleams; there is the couch and it comforts; gentle is the comforting but the hour is fleeting. And that flash of the golden couch is compared to lightning. It takes place in a moment, in the twinkling of an eye, as the last trumpet calls. The last trumpet

2 Co 3:17

calls when truth is made known no longer by the written page but by its own Presence, when man becomes a pupil of God,* when after the discourses of apostles and prophets, the Son of God, the Word of the Father, speaks last of all in his own Person. This trumpet cannot sound a hesitant note: it summons only to a solemnity, only at the new moon, and at the dawning of a new day.

Jo 6:45

5. *Do you 'blow for us on the trumpet', good Jesus, 'at the new moon, at the festival of our solemnity'.** Truly it is a festival, when you reveal your divine Majesty. Nothing is more festal but nothing is briefer. A day I call it; it is but an hour, an hour truly festal and truly solemn. *Reveal in us, good Jesus, some hours of that eternal day.** You will at once turn from night into day anyone to whom you reveal the word of your light, for you are eternal day. *Flash upon us such lightning as this.** Anyone on whom your lightning flashes becomes a flash of lightning. Anyone on whom you shed a ray of your light, you make like yourself. 'We shall be like him', says John, 'when he appears.'* Mountains which you touch with such a ray do not smoulder but sparkle.* They become golden, on whom your gold reflects. Your head of finest gold does not discover a couch of gold but where it reclines creates a couch of gold.

Ps 80:4

Ps 18:3

Ps 143:6

1 Jn 3:2
Ps 103:32

Then that verse of Luke is no longer appropriate: 'The Son of Man has nowhere to lay his head.' Do you see, Lord Jesus, how many golden couches you have here? Never does the head of your Majesty recline more gladly than on the golden bosom of virginity. Look upon these virginal breasts, breasts reserved for you. Upon these you frequently recline and rest and sleep at midday, in some golden calm of your clear light. Not here do foxes have their dens; not here do birds of heaven build their nests.* This couch is too solid for the crafty fox to be able to burrow here. No room is left for heretical guile, where clear truth flashes in the sky. It is too lofty for either the crafty fox or the proud peacock to be able to reach.⁴ These things are hidden 'from the wise and prudent and revealed to little ones',* who

Lk 9:58

Mt 11:25

follow the lowly ascent, 'the purple ascent',* and tread in the footsteps of the passion of Christ. Deep purple is the ascent which the blood of Christ has sealed and the loyalty of his passion dyed purple.

Sg 3:10

6. But one should observe the way, the harmonious way, in which the silver pillars and the purple steps blend together. In the pillars you relish the wisdom of faith; in the ascent you embrace it with humility. The pillars represent meditation, the ascent imitation. For the Kingdom of God exists not in words alone but in virtue. What will you say about his example, if you regard humiliation as servitude? She is no maidservant whom the royal purple ennobles. Purple indeed is the emblem of royalty. If you either disdain or dread these steps, observe that they are purple. Humility worn for Christ manifests a royal dignity. But, O bride of Christ, tread the purple steps with feet snow-white! Noble is the path which your Beloved trod before you. For how beautiful are the purple steps which Christ with sacred tread sealed before you with his holy feet, feet to which no dust adhered!* Snow-white feet which he sealed with the imprint of his Blood. Passionately retrace these footsteps! Slip from your feet the shoes of the flesh!* Holy indeed is the ascent you prepare for yourself. Climb these steps barefoot and unshod. This purple was dyed not by the blood of a shellfish but by the blood of Christ. Here gladly set your foot, that your foot may be dyed in the blood of Christ. Let not the foot of pride overtake you, if you would follow the humble ascent which is sealed with the sacred blood of your Bridegroom. With this blood dye not only your foot but also your hand and your head, that you may ascend wholly purple, wholly royal and wholly ennobled by the passion of Christ.

Lk 10:11

Ex 3:5

If you share his passion, you share his Kingdom. Do not think yourself renowned by noble birth in the world. You will be the more a serf, if you show respect for that, if you boast of your gentility of birth to your Bridegroom, if because of worldly pomp you prefer yourself to others or suppose you are entitled to some privileged position. Contrary to the humility of your resolve, you are stripping yourself of Christ's glory, thanks to your family lineage, if you expect to be ennobled by anything else. Let his purple be pomp enough for you, ascent enough, glory enough, that 'you may glory only in the Cross of your Lord Jesus Christ'.* The purple ascent will lead you to the couch of gold, for the grace of contemplation is reserved to the humble and peaceful.* It is 'hidden from the wise and prudent, to be revealed to little ones'.† This purple is a great pledge of the love which your Beloved offered you. Truly a great pledge of love is his suffering unto death. 'Greater love than this no man has, that he lay down his life for his friends.'* Such was the pledge he offered; such a pledge your own passion, your own humiliation claims in turn. Let your memory recall what he endured for you and how deeply he loved a bride for whom he suffered such humiliation. Love him then who first and foremost loved you so much more. Our times no longer demand that you pour out your blood. Pour out your soul, 'pour out your heart like water'.* For though you surrender your body to be burned, if you have not charity, what does it profit you?* At the end of our text, as a climactic bond of all the graces, charity is enthroned and the centre is said to be inlaid with charity, as if with an ornament, 'for the sake of the daughters of Jerusalem'.*

margin:
Ga 6:14
Jm 4:6; see Leclercq, 'Otia Monastica', 107:32
†Mt 11:25
Jn 15:13
Lm 2:19
1 Co 13:3
Sg 3:10

NOTES ON SERMON EIGHTEEN

1. G. seems to have composed S 18 for one individual and then to have adapted it for a convent of nuns. He uses the plural of address in the first and last sentences of par. 1, throughout par. 2, and in the last part of par. 5. In S 17, given to nuns, he promised a talk on this subject. He ends S 18 without the usual prayer and continues easily into S 19, just as he will end S 20 and continue into S 21, so that S 18-19, and S 20-21, should be considered in pairs.
2. See White, 72-74 for sheep, and 165-7 for serpents.
3. See White 53-4 foxes, 149 for peacock's, G's *superba volucris.*

SERMON 19
FOUNDATION AND CROWN

Charity is the foundation, center, and crown of the virtues. 1. Charity is set in the center as a gem common to all virtues and the crown of the whole carriage. 2. Love ever new to match the Lord's is like overflowing oil and like wine ever fermenting. 3-4. Charity shares its possessions without boasting, envy, detraction, or calumny. 5-6. Charity casts out fear of punishment, fear of giving offence, but not reverential fear. 7-8. What is reverential fear and how does it differ from charity?

HE INLAID THE CENTER WITH CHARITY FOR THE SAKE OF THE DAUGHTERS OF JERUSALEM*[1]   *Sg 3:10*

You desire to hear something new, but I have no news except that love should renew you. This commandment is the news I give you;* nothing is more known *Jo 13:34* to you yet nothing is more new. You are not unskilled and untried in this craft. This is your particular duty. Indeed you have been consecrated especially for the commerce of love. According to our text also, for your sake the center of Solomon's carriage is said to be inlaid with charity. 'He inlaid the center with charity', says the text, 'for the sake of the daughters of Jerusalem.' As if by a special perogative this verse has delegated to you the practice of love. 'Strive after the better gifts',* daughters *1 Co 12:31* of Jerusalem, but especially that you may love. Love towers above every grace and in the description of such a carriage charity is put at the top as the crown and culmination of the other graces. Many graces are enumerated in this carriage, but all come to a peak in charity. Charity is the summit as charity is the foundation. That you may be 'rooted and grounded in charity', is Paul's prayer.* Charity exists with the first graces, with the last, and with the graces inlaid between. Charity initiates and crowns and shares with the other gifts; hence it is set in the center as a gem common to all and the crown of the whole carriage. Both the color of purple and the gleam of gold would be duller, if not graced with charity. How great is its grace, since it gives brilliance to the very gold of contemplation! It is the center and, as it were, the marrow of the other graces. No other virtue is so intimate, none so penetrates and permeates the spirit and so fills the nooks and crannies of the heart. Love seeps into the very marrow of the spirit and flows into its hidden veins. 'Charity in the center', says the verse. It is aptly in the center, since it is so intimate.

Eph 3:17

The fulness of the law is charity.* So the law is empty, if forsaken by charity. Charity is an artery which gives life to the law and to the other virtues. The others restrict themselves, as it were, to some part; charity is common to every level. Whether you are carried out of your mind or whether you return to your right senses, everywhere the practice of charity is both necessary and pleasant. The duties of the other graces are diversified and they work in shifts, but the command of charity, as it were, holds the tiller without relief. 'If we are carried out of our mind, it is for God, and if we return to our right senses, the charity of Christ impels us.'* The charity of Christ, in my opinion, really compels you. Towards what does it compel you? Towards itself. Other people have other duties; your special function is love.* Love is a shameless champion of its own cause and love exercises a gentle tyranny over its victims. Love is always driving itself on to greater heights.

Rm 13:10

2 Co 5:13-14

Lam 14, n. 53

2. 'Strive then for the better gifts',* daughters of Jerusalem, but especially that you may love. Let this striving ever impel you forward. Let this command-

1 Co 12:31

ment ever be new for you. And new it is, unless in your affections sweet Jesus has grown old. May he always be young in you and may the lapse of time in no way lessen his grace. Yes, your Jesus is young in you. He is always new, but he is not a strange God. Truly new is he for whom you always sigh with restless love. In a word, you have only one longing, that he may please you ever more! How much does one please, when one cannot please enough? By no means can you be pleasing to yourselves more than if he is pleasing to you.

He wants your spirit and seeks nothing else. Your spirit alone is sufficient, but only if it is wholly surrendered. Your spirit alone is enough considering your capacity, but too little considering his deserts. If you compare yourself with yourself and measure yourself in your own scale, total surrender is enough; yet if you pour yourself out, nothing remains for yourself. Whereas if you should weigh yourself by his measure and, as it were, set yourself in his scales, what counterweight will you have opposite him? If your love checks and restrains itself beneath your capacity it fails in the scale; even if it pours itself out to capacity, it is but slight. What then can you do? Are you to strain yourself beyond your capacity in a vain effort? Why not? Love seeks no cure for the impossible. No tasks are great enough for love, provided love itself has not become lukewarm. How will love be miserly with its own possessions, when it is trustworthy with another's? How will love be prodigal in its duties, but miserly in itself? Love spends nothing more gladly than itself; it can spend nothing more prodigally.

What prodigality is greater than when nothing is kept in reserve? Love boils over, does not contain itself, overflows itself, rivals immensity, while it knows not how to set a limit to its affections. It is oil which cannot stop its flow until no other container is available, except that not even then can it be checked.* *2 K 4:6* Love shows a characteristic of new wine which, by fermenting as it is born and by wantonness as it ages, bubbles up and overflows unable to contain itself, always seething and fermenting with fresh affection. In its infirmity, love does not excuse but accuses itself. Nothing is enough for love, nothing less than itself. Love cannot be satisfied with itself and yet love can feed only on itself; it is food delicious enough for itself. Love wants nothing more than to love. What will a person give in exchange for love? What will one give or what will one receive? Nothing is imparted more graciously than love, nothing is experienced more gently. Love is delicious in desire and in enjoyment; love is delicious in joy and sorrow. Truly love is sweet and only love is sweet and all love is sweet but no love exists to compare with the love of Christ, for his beauty is above all beauty.

'Above all beauty', says Solomon, 'I have loved Wisdom.'* How is he not handsome, who is the 'brightness of eternal light'?* 'My brother Jonathan',* how lovable you are and how very handsome! I intended to say 'Jesus', but from force of habit I pronounced the name Jonathan. Yet this is a graceful error, because it did express a grace. The error was in name only, for in fact the real meaning of his name was kept. 'Jonathan' means 'gift of a dove' and designates one who is full of spiritual grace, the child who has been given to us.* Whether I say Jonathan or Jesus, I understand Jesus. How lovable are you, my brother Jonathan, and how very handsome! Do you think it presumption for me to call him brother? These words echo not my rashness but his love. It would be presumption had he himself not encouraged my audacity. He himself assumed the character and showed the affection of this relationship and according to the apostle: 'He does not blush to call us brothers.'* If he does not blush, why should you not also say confidently: 'my brother Jonathan', or if you prefer to use his familiar name: my brother Jesus, you are lovable and very handsome, 'you are lovable beyond the love of women'!* Your desires for Christ, holy women, burn with a restless and passionate affection, but he is much more lovable than he is loved by you.

3. 'Strive then for the better gifts'*, but especially that you may love. The text enumerates the wood of

Lebanon, the silver pillars, the golden canopy, the purple steps and finally crowns all with charity. What else could it do? 'I show you', says St Paul, 'a still more excellent way.'* Good indeed are silver pillars and great surely is the grace of God's word. But 'if I should speak with the tongues of men and of angels but have not charity, I have become like a clashing cymbal',* relaying the hollow sound of a voice without the feeling of charity. Mighty is the glory of the golden couch by which you are to understand the secrets of the mysteries. But what follows? 'If I should understand the secrets of the mysteries and all knowledge but have not charity, I am nothing.'* Do you ascend the purple steps and rejoice in having the emblem of Christ's passion? 'But if I deliver my body to be burned but have not charity, it profits me nothing', the apostle says.*

1 Co 12:31

1 Co 13:1

1 Co 13:2

1 Co 13:3

'Charity is not puffed up, is not ambitious, does not seek its own way'*: it rejoices in the center and has volunteered its property for common use. For 'the center was inlaid with charity'. 'It is not boastful', says Paul, 'not ambitious'. For charity knows nothing of private property. It is not the way of charity to love the private property it has or to long for what it has not. It does not wish to excel others, nor even to have a greater possession of goodness itself. Many acknowledge the weaknesses of their own merits. Therefore entertaining no lofty opinion of themselves, though they are not boastful, perhaps they are ambitious. Though they have no grounds for boastfulness, boastful enough is their desire to have grounds for boastfulness. These also love their own excellence, as long as they either desire its realization or mope and pine because it can not be realized. But charity does not make a travelling companion of moping envy; charity does not seek what is its own, so how could it purloin what belongs to another?

1 Co 13:4

4. Why do you wish through envy to ruin another's good? Will you add to yourself what you take from another? Perhaps so, if it is material wealth you steal. Among persons in cloister, I do not fear rapacity of this kind. There is a more subtle kind of

rapacity rooted in envy. Why do you not consider it rapacity if you spare someone's purse but steal his good name? You do not covet his possessions but you do tear his reputation to shreds. What gain does detraction of another confer upon you? If you carp at good qualities, what accrues to you from that? Perhaps on the manifest truth of another's virtue your teeth are being ground away in your mouth after you sharpened them for calumny. You dare not gnaw away at another and yet you cannot join in his praise. Because you no longer cheat him of his reputation by your words, are you therefore not robbing him? How is this not robbery, when you defraud evident goodness of its deserved tribute and when without spoiling by falsehood another's real worth, you suppress it by silence? Are you interested in hearing that there is robbery even in mere evaluation? 'He did not regard it as robbery', says the apostle, 'that he be equal to God.'* A fair evaluation of another's good qualities cannot be conceived in an envious soul. For the envious soul refuses to think that another is acting well; although the envious person dare not object openly, within himself he either ignores or minimizes the other's merits. Why is that, if not because spite, while always thinking of its own excellence, casts a shadow over another's excellence?

Ph 2:6

'But charity thinks no evil, does not rejoice over inequity' and, if I may say so, over inequality, 'but rejoice with the truth'.* It does not think of private gain; it rejoices in what is in the center and common to all. It does not seek its own interests but those of Christ Jesus. In everyone, it either loves or desires His glory. Christ is common to all, for he is the Mediator* and therefore things which are not in the center but confine themselves to a part, are not his.² Why do you wish through spite to restrict Christ to a part? Do you want the grace of the Spirit to be miserly? Do you want his blessings restricted to you alone? Allow the Spirit of the Lord to spread and overflow and pour itself out over all flesh and fill the universe. Do not imprison within the narrow limits of your heart a generosity which is common to all.

1 Co 13:5-6

1 Tm 2:5

The Spirit bestows his riches upon all,* and do you attempt to diminish the affluence of grace and reduce its immensity to pettiness? Christ scorns the miserly confines of an envious heart. His goodness cannot be held back by your jealousy. His goodness flows freely; its oil pours itself not only into you but also into neighboring vessels. Insure that they be yours in turn. They will be yours surely, if you rejoice in the common good.³ Otherwise you are emptying your own soul of oil and Christ the Mediator is none the less poured into others. Therefore he wishes that what belongs to him should be in the center. 'By this,' he says, 'shall all men know that you are my disciples, if you have love for one another.'*

Rm 10:12

Jn 13:35

5. Do you see how charity is the special emblem of discipleship in Christ and the singular mark of his teaching?⁴ Consequently charity is introduced here in the final place as an adornment of the other graces. 'He inlaid the center with charity.' O how soft is the inlay of charity. Charity for one's neighbor knows no spite; charity towards the Lord knows no fear. Charity involves no punishment but fear involves punishment; therefore 'there is no fear in charity, while perfect charity casts out fear'.* For what will charity fear? Old offences? But 'charity covers a multitude of sins'.* Will the weakness of one's own conscience fear lest it fall?* 'But love is strong as death.'* Charity casts out both kinds of fear. Yet neither will perfect charity fear temporal hardships for the sake of Christ. Indeed not even if hardships are eternal can consummate love be wearied and grow faint. Love cannot fail to take delight in such sweetness, once love has experienced such sweetness. Charity does not love in order to escape perdition; charity prefers to be cast out and as a punishment perish for eternity, rather than to be deprived of the exercise of eternal love. For 'if a man should give all his property' for charity, 'he would regard it as nothing'.*

1 Jn 4:18

1 Pet 4:8
1 Co 8:10-11
Sg 8:6

Sg 8:7

Truly this inlay is soft, for even amid insults one can rest upon it with as much delight as holiness. Grant me, good Jesus, that upon this inlay I may be mindful of you and meditate upon you in the night-watches.* Sheer delight is the memory which love inlays; welcome is the meditation which charity suggests.* For every thought about Christ is delightful and welcome. Love of one's neighbor involves compassion and some taste of fears, while it knows how to grieve with those who mourn. But in what way can you share mourning over Christ? Even 'if he was crucified out of weakness, yet he lives by the power of God'.* Everywhere he affords you grounds not for suffering but for rejoicing together with him.* He is wholly attractive, wholly inlaid with longing and charity. For what will you observe in Christ, which does not both manifest his charity towards us and prompt ours in return? He is wholly an enticement to charity for us and a provocation to love. He leaves no place in himself for the sentiment of fear. He wholly desires to be loved, as he wholly deserves to be loved. Do not look back upon torments, O virgin, when such great charms are set before you in your Bridegroom. Fear should be laid to rest where so many signs of love catch the eye. Charity disdains all traffic with fear; charity cannot be coerced, just as it cannot be constrained.

6. Therefore 'perfect charity casts out fear' as useless and superfluous, but not that chastened fear which endures forever and ever.* There is indeed a fear which charity sends packing, a fear which truth sends as a messenger, and a fear which both charity and truth send as a visitor. The first fear is cautious, the second is chaste but does not endure forever and ever, the third is both chaste and enduring. The first fears punishment, the second fears giving offence, the third is a reverence fully liberated and carefree. Even the first fears giving offence, but for fear of punishment; the second fears giving offence, but for fear of giving offence. Indeed justice is somehow insulted if, through fear of punishment, justice finds favor. Justice in itself is sufficiently deserving to attract men's attention to itself and to win their affections. This fear then perfect charity banishes. For how is charity perfect, if it needs the spur of fear

to cultivate justice? Perfect love possesses the mind without reservation, desirous that all the functions of justice be delegated to itself alone. Fear is ice-cold and drags its feet, content merely to escape punishment. Love knows no aversion; it is fervent and stretches forward to what lies ahead; fear is more withdrawn and undertakes the obligations of justice only under compulsion.

Perfect love owes all its action to justice alone, leaving fear no claim upon justice. How could it be otherwise? Does not justice win for itself enough merit for every good work? Yes, Christ for us was made justice.* What then? Does Christ not have in himself sufficient endowment to be pleasing? Does he then also need another's assistance to be pleasing? If we do not surrender to him for his own sake alone, how will our love of him be perfect? *I will love you, good Jesus. I will love you, my strength, whom I cannot love without your help and cannot love as you deserve. May my endeavors be directed to you without reserve and may they not be diverted and distracted by any other affection. But even when totally directed toward you, how feeble are our endeavors! How then shall I weaken what is so feeble even at full strength? May I be wholly carried to you by my desires, good God. Draw me to yourself that I may require no stimulus of fear and that perfect charity may banish any recourse to fear.*

*Rm 3:22;
1 Co 6:11*

7. What follows? Are eternal torments not to be feared? Obviously they are to be feared and avoided 'for no one ever hated his own flesh'.* But a more passionate love of Christ does not need the motive of fear to be attracted to justice. Such love fears nothing so much as giving offence, precisely because it offends, not because it will be punished. But this holds true as long as human affairs hang in the balance, as long as praise is not assured to man in his own lifetime. But when after his lifetime a man is introduced to truth, thereafter fear of this kind will cease, giving place to a third fear which though it succeeds the first two is never superseded, since it endures for ever and ever. The first fear then dreads lest it pay for its

Eph 5:20

rashness in giving offence; the second dreads lest in its weakness it give offence; the third has nothing to dread. For what is to be dreaded by complete happiness and consummate charity?

This last fear springs from the nursery of charity. I dare not affirm yet I dare not deny that it is charity. For what else but love is that affection trying to be, since it now knows not the passion of fear? How is that not love which already has almost ceased to be fear? What is the logic of a fear which dreads nothing? A fear so secure I would honor with the name love, except that God himself loves us in the afterlife, yet in such Majesty there is no place for fear. But in ourselves how shall that fear be distinguished from charity? And in the afterlife what else is fearing but not waxing proud against the Lord of majesty? What is that fear but willing subjection, obedience without coercion, reverence voluntarily offered? How is that fear, which is not afraid of giving offence? Indeed it is incapable of giving offence. But again, how is that not fear, which does not dare to give offence? So it seems in one respect not to be fear, because it has no dread of sin or danger, and in another respect to be fear, because it ventures upon nothing bold or rash.

What is that fear but humble reverence, offered of necessity because it is due but suffering no constraint of necessity? Our obligation to worship exists by reason of our creaturehood but our freedom to love does not advert to an obligation. What is that fear but a lack of temerity and negligence rather than the coercion of obligation? Do you see how closely this fear approximates charity? It is almost but not quite charity. It differs from charity in its cause but it is equal in its affection. Do you ask for what cause it differs? It differs because an inferior creature must observe every nod of a Majesty so great. This obligation is incumbent upon you in justice, but charity does not look to that motive; charity is carried away by admiration for the divine Majesty without a glance at its own lowly rank. Therefore that motive which fear respects, charity disregards, for charity is compelled by more powerful motives.

8. In their motives then, fear and love differ, though they are akin in obedience and freedom of affection. So the first fear dreads punishment; the second deprivation; the third dreads neither. The first, perfect charity banishes; the second charity tolerates for an interval; the third charity makes its inseparable companion. This third fear, daughters of Jerusalem, you must capture. Beware of the first, which charity sends packing: 'He inlaid the center with charity.' In mentioning the center he intends the whole to be understood. Let charity inlay, let charity clothe the center of your heart. This is your wedding dress and this your dowry. If this is demanded of a wedding guest, how much more will be expected of a bride? Charity desires to occupy ahead of time and possess all the corners of your mind alone. Do not share them with a degenerate and foreign affection. The inlay of charity is soft and delicate; not even for an instant is it willing to be offended by a disagreeable fear. 'For the sake of the daughters of Jerusalem', our text continues. And rightly, since 'peace is universal for those who love your law'.* *Ps 118:165*

If anyone takes pride in grace conferred, how much more should you! For although it is granted that the wealth of spiritual gifts is great, still charity surpasses them all. Charity not only surpasses, it includes them all. Charity is both delightful and wealthy. Then as the psalm states, it is 'amid the chosen lots'* of the virtues and in the communion of spiritual graces that one sleeps on the inlay of charity. Being in the center charity shares with all and being better than all, draws all the virtues to a peak. 'Strive then for the better gifts',* daughters of Jerusalem, but especially that you may have charity and have it more abundantly;* pass wholly into the affection of love, for wholly lovable is our Beloved, Jesus Christ, who lives and reigns forever and ever. Amen.

Ps 67:14

1 Co 12:31

2 Co 2:4

NOTES ON SERMON NINETEEN

1. G. seems to have written this to one individual but to have adapted it for a congregation of nuns: *vos . . . dedicatae,* 1; *sanctae mulieres,* last sentence, par. 2; *vos, filiae Jerusalem,* 8; Notice however: *pro viribus tuis,* par. 2; *tibi,* par. 3; *tu,* par. 4; *vides,* par. 5; *vides,* par. 6.
2. On this par. see Lam 17, nn. 71, 72; 18, n. 77.
3. Read *laetata* for *laetatus* to agree with *virgo* at the end of par. 5, despite Mab., Migne, mss Paris 9605 and Troyes 419.
4. Reading *indicium* for *iudicium,* with Migne, mss Paris 9605 and Troyes 419.

SERMON 20
AFFECTIVE CONTEMPLATION

The bride contemplates affectively his cross and his crown. 1. The daughters of Sion are invited to Solomon's wedding; 2. they are invited to contemplation gradually; 3. the cloistered are invited but must not go unescorted. 4. The whole life of the Beloved is a passionate invitation; 5. exhalted mysteries invite the exalted; humbler mysteries, especially his passion, invite all. 6. The cross of his historical body was also his crown; 7. the circle of believers, especially the cloistered, must be a crown not of thorns but of pure gold. 8. A crown is a continuous circle in unity elevated in hope; you are united in the flesh in this circle of the Church, and she is united in the Spirit with her Bridegroom. 9. Rejoice, O faithful soul; rejoice, O chosen bride, with your Bridegroom rejoicing in this espousal. 10. O bridegroom, engrave these mysteries on our stony hearts.

GO FORTH AND BEHOLD KING SOLOMON IN THE DIADEM WITH WHICH HIS MOTHER CROWNED HIM ON THE DAY OF HIS WEDDING, ON THE DAY OF HIS GLADNESS OF HEART*[1] *Sg 3:11*

You have heard whither the daughters of Sion have been invited, but you have not yet heard whence they are bidden go forth. That the text does not explain. Whence then is it? From Sion? But 'the God of gods will be seen in Sion'.* Not from Sion then are the daughters called whom the text summons to see God. Are they summoned perhaps not to the sight of God but to see 'Solomon in the diadem with which his mother crowned him'? Then there is no difficulty in bidding a daughter of Sion go forth from Sion. But was Solomon not born in Sion? Therefore if they are summoned from Sion, they are only summoned to Sion, from the upper Sion to the lower Sion. For it seems²* neither worthy nor consistent that the daughters of Sion should depart from Sion, especially to see him whose dwelling-place is in Sion and who was born there.³ I remember the explanation of an eloquent and learned man when treating this passage: 'Those who are bidden go forth, seem to be in the wrong place.'³ What he said suited the occasion well enough; he directed his comment to the advantage of his audience. To me, however, the daughters to whom these words of exhortation are addressed seem to be well placed. Where is that you ask. Upon the golden couch, the subject of yesterday's sermon. It is a delightful place and productive of more joyfulness than human affection can conceive. The excess of delight exhausts itself and overflowing pleasure drains the spirit. This joy is intermittent; it cannot be continuous, because it is excessive. Yet those interruptions are good, when there is no parting from the Bridegroom. It is not given to anyone who is dwelling in the flesh to possess the golden couch as an inheritance. So the daughters of Sion are bidden go forth, but as if one cautioned them: 'Do not go too far off.'

2. 'Go forth', says the text, 'and behold King Solomon in the diadem with which his mother crowned him.' The speaker does not wish the daughters to part from Christ, whether they experience a transport of mind or whether they return to sobriety.* A good sobriety is simplicity of faith, for the gaze of the beholders can endure it and be encouraged by it. Happy the one who in descending is welcomed on this level of faith and who in

ascending begins on this level. Indeed this is the first stage of contemplation encountered by those who are ascending. Eagerness for contemplation is good, but knowledge is necessary. You are ready and robed to set out for that golden couch, a place designed for contemplation. I approve your enthusiasm, but wait while I show you the steps and set the pace. The golden couch is a lookout and a very lofty lookout, soaring above all the clouds of earthly vapor. With your inexperience, why are you ready to make one leap to the top? Get down on your hands and knees, like the lizard in Proverbs,* that you may learn to frequent the palace of King Solomon. For the present crawl, until you are swept upwards. For the psalm says that 'he has prepared ascents', not leaps, 'in his heart'.* The time will come, however, when the ascent will be changed into a leap or rather into an assumption. What are these ascents but purifications of the mind? Hence they occur 'in the vale of tears',* because transgressions washed with tears are purged. Happy the one who has shed tears enough in the little bed of his heart, who has lamented enough, whose sorrow has reached the brim, for whose consolation divine inspiration whispers to summon him from the vale of tears, whose eye is not disturbed by the fury of the Judge, that he may bravely gaze upon King Solomon with tranquil countenance 'on the day when joy gladdens his heart'.

Pr 30:28

Ps 83:6. Lam 183, n. 86

Ps 83:7. Lam 193, n. 155

3. 'Go forth, daughters of Sion, and behold King Solomon.' They are indeed held worthy of this joyful vision who have cloistered themselves under a penitential rule and confined themselves by the observance of discipline, 'whose soul refuses to be consoled'.* Would you learn how good seclusion is? 'A garden enclosed, a fountain sealed.'*[4] 'Arise, hasten, my love, and come.'* Do you see now how he invites and calls his love, because she knows how to cloister herself? But if you have been daughters cloistered, refuse to come forth until Christ invites you. Dinah came forth unescorted; she came forth to see not King Solomon but the women of that district.* You know what she found. As for you,

Ps 76:3
Sg 4:12
Sg 2:10

Gn 34:1

refuse to go forth, except when either the Bridegroom or his companions invite you. Lazarus came forth when the Lord recalled him to life.* Noah went forth from the ark, a cloister which kept him unharmed from the billows of this world; but he disembarked when the Lord opened the hatches for him.* Abraham emigrated from his own land to see the land of promise; but he emigrated in obedience to a call.* You also come forth, daughters of Sion, invited to the grace of a happier vision. Imprisoned and woefully imprisoned is one who neither endeavors nor deserves to come forth to this blessed vision. To be imprisoned is the lot of a slave; to go forth is the lot of the free. In Paul's words, when you 'turn to the Lord, the veil will be removed', the veil of ignorance and ignobility; for 'the Lord is the Spirit. Where the Spirit of the Lord is, there is freedom'.* Where there is greater abundance of spirit, there is more plentiful freedom. Whatever is imprisoned and wrapped in a winding cloth has little freedom to breathe.

Jn 11:43-44

Gn 8:16

Gn 12:1

2 Co 3:16-17

4. Go forth then, daughters of Sion, that with Paul you may be able to say: 'But we all, with faces unveiled, reflecting as in a mirror the glory of the Lord, are being transformed into his very image.'* The vision of God is always to be welcomed with affection. And truly effective and passionate is the vision of yourself, good Jesus, which carries off the affections of those who gaze upon it. Did Moses not suffer some gentle passion in his longing to cross over and see that great vision?* Would you like to hear how effective it is? 'When I am lifted up from the earth, I will draw all things to myself.'* But when you are humbled to the earth, do you not draw all spirits to yourself? For my part, good Jesus, I do not await the glory of your resurrection nor save my wonder for your power as you ascend into heaven; from the very beginning of your annunciation or of your nativity the angelic voices ring in my ears, the new tale amazes me, and the unwonted light risen in the darkness sweeps me towards itself.

2 Co 3:18

Ex 3:3

Jn 12:32

A naked vision, one which does not translate

itself into worthy affections, should be lumped with ignorance and blindness. Would you welcome an example of a fruitful vision? 'The islands saw and trembled and the ends of the earth were amazed and drew near', says Isaiah.* You see what a harvest of virtues the vision of God begets: fear, amazement, love. 'They saw', says Isaiah, 'and trembled; they were amazed and drew near.' 'They saw' you so as to understand, 'they trembled' so as to revere you, 'they were amazed' at the novelty, 'they drew near' in conformity. Vision comprehends, fear restrains, amazement stuns, drawing near seizes and unites. Yes, they draw near, who are enflamed with zeal. Fear humbles, amazement infatuates, as it were, but love melds the spirit of the one who sees.

Is 41:5

Vain is the vision and unworthy of the name of contemplation, which is not clothed in such affections. Or will you admit[5] that he has a vision, who as a result of his knowledge of the mystery does not fear, is not amazed, is not on fire? The spirit is sobered by fear, absorbed in amazement, and by drawing near is engrafted and united. The grace of contemplation is consistent with such virtues but especially with amazement and love. For in amazement and wonder, the mind goes out of itself, but in love it approaches the divine. Nor should the value of contemplation be judged so much by its subject-matter as by its manner. Both should be considered: the kinds of truths to be contemplated and the degree of their affections. But it is more satisfying to be more deeply affected in contemplating a less exalted truth than to be less affected in contemplating a higher truth. This vision is hidden 'from the wise and prudent' and revealed 'to little ones'.* Hence Isaiah says: 'The ends of the earth were amazed and drew near.'

Mt 11:25

5. What the humble are able to grasp, usually arouses greater affections and conveys an admiration and love of itself. 'When I am lifted up from the earth', says the Lord, 'I will draw all things to myself.'* Everything in you, good Jesus, has a power of attraction and stirs the thoughtful to affection;

Jn 12:32

but not all of us can reach all mysteries. Exalted mysteries are for the exalted only; humbler mysteries are for all. What greater humility exists than to be exalted on a cross? Of this also the Lord says: 'When I am lifted up from the earth, I will draw all things to myself.'* Such humility does not fail to attract. But why not? Who would not be filled with amazement and ecstasy at the mere thought of this event? Whose affection would faith in this event not exhaust and make giddy and render helpless? Here is a scene easy to contemplate but abounding in grace. The simplicity of such faith has less understanding but a great incentive to admiration and love. Here is a scene accessible to all, which gives birth to the sweetest of transports. Do not disdain this scene for contemplation. It is not difficult to recall and it is rich in glory. 'Far be it from me to glory', says Paul, 'except in the cross of our Lord Jesus Christ.'* Now what more do you wish to hear? The cross itself is the crown of glory, the diadem of the kingdom.* On the cross Christ triumphed, despoiling princes and powers and banishing the prince of this world. Glorious is the vision of his triumph.

6. 'Go forth, daughters of Sion, and behold King Solomon in the diadem with which his mother crowned him.' See the flesh which he took from the human race, triumphing on the wood. Happy the flesh which Christ took to himself not as a prison cell but as a crown, for it served him not as a burden but as a badge. All of us have been concealed in the flesh as if in prison cells, shackled and enslaved to the law of sin. 'Unhappy man that I am!' says Paul. 'Who will deliver me from the body of this death? The grace of God through Jesus Christ.'* For 'by sending his Son in the likeness of sinful flesh as a sin offering, God condemned sin in the flesh'.* Authentic flesh in Christ, not feeling the weight of sin, carried to us all the palm of victory over sin. Fittingly is his imaculate body understood as a diadem, the body of his triumph, the body of his honor and glory, the body in whose blood the hand-written bond of sin is blotted out,* the charter of justice and salvation

signed, and the wedding contracts settled. Scripturally, this is the day of betrothal when, rejecting the ancient rites, Christ instituted the new sacraments of the Church, when as a sign of unending matrimony and nuptial union, a blending of blood and water flowed from his side. Today he gave the Synagogue a writ of divorce and from his former spouse now full of hate, he passed to his later and beloved bride. He passed from an old to a new bride, whom he presented to himself 'glorious, without spot or wrinkle or any such blemish'.* The sign of her newness is that she is without wrinkle. Christ smoothed out the wrinkles of the letter and drew forth the newness within it. Why, O daughters of Sion and of the Synagogue, do you seek to restore the wrinkles which Christ smoothed out? When the new supersede, why continue to take pride in the old? 'Emerge, daughters of Sion', from the labyrinth of the letter, from an interpretation narrow and obscure. 'Emerge and behold King Solomon with the diadem with which his mother crowned him.' The incarnation which you regard as contumely, for us is a crown. Behold at last how he blessed 'the crown of the year of his bounty, how his fields have been filled with fruitfulness'.*   *Eph 5:27*

Ps 64:12

Behold the crown; behold also the harvest—a crown of victory, a harvest of virtues. Whence comes the harvest, if not because the grain of wheat fell into the ground and died?* Again 'this is the victory which overcomes the world, our faith'.* And the host of believers is itself a crown and an adornment for Christ. 'You shall be a crown of glory in the hand of the Lord', says Isaiah, 'and a diadem of the kingdom in the hand of your God.'* Do you appropriate these words to yourselves? Or is the name of God not blasphemed through you? 'Emerge, daughters of Sion', and behold how glorious God is in his saints, in the hope perhaps that this vision may provoke you to emulation and make you pass from your loneliness to the companionship of the Church. Even if you were a spouse abandoned, now, however, Isaiah continues, 'you shall no longer be called "forsaken" nor   *Jn 12:24*
1 Jn 5:4

Is 62:3

Is 62:4 your land "desolate" '.*

7. But now let us cease addressing ourselves to outsiders. Let us rather take pleasure ourselves in beholding how the oases of the desert are already growing fertile, how Christ in his Church wears a crown of believers. 'What is our hope' and 'our crown *1 Th 2:19* of glory? Is it not you, before the Lord.'* If Paul says this, should Christ not say it even more? 'As I live', says the Lord, 'you shall be arrayed with them all as *Is 49:18* with an ornament.'* Have you noticed⁶ how the ranks of believers are described as an ornament of Christ in the Church? Why are they not also a crown? Above other ornaments, a crown manifests a striking and brilliant dignity, for while other ornaments are for the body, a crown is for the head. The occasions on which the crown is worn enhance this dignity; it is reserved for solemn festivals.

I see that your interest is at last aroused; now you are referring to yourselves the interpretation of this word.⁷ In the right to a crown you already see your own prerogative, because you are drawn together by the profession of a purer life, schooled in its practice, unflagging in enthusiasm for it and exultant in its peace.⁸ Rightly are they considered entitled to the diadem who are no longer called to arms but rather celebrate a triumph, whose 'joust is no longer against flesh and blood', who no longer eye the head *Eph 6:12,* of a serpent but adorn the head of Christ.* You are *Nb 21:7-9* Christ's crown and joy and therefore, as you have begun, so stand firm, most dearly beloved, 'so stand *Ph 4:1* firm in the Lord' or rather so encircle the Lord.*

Yours is a lofty position; carry there no cheaper *1 Co 1:26* material. 'Consider your own calling';* consider to what service you have been elevated. Do not weave any 'hay, wood or straw' into the Lord's diadem, nothing in a word which might either deserve or *1 Co 3:12-13* dread the fire.* Tangled thorns may be burnt in the *Is 33:12* fire.* 'Do not rival evildoers'† or envy those who set *†Ps 36:1* a crown of thorns on the head of our King. Such a diadem brings not honor but horror. Christ has a greater horror of harsh manners and sharp tongues than of the pricks of thorns, especially in people who have been called to the simplicity of silence, to the commerce of charity, to the repose of leisure, to the school of humility, to a vow of obedience and to the bond of unity.⁹ But it is not a good bond when people plot together and form a ring to disparage others, saying after the fashion of the Jews: Let us do away with 'the just one, because he is obnoxious to us and opposes our actions'.* But always court the blessing of peace from a good motive.*

Ws 2:12
Ga 4:18

8. Then again the shape of a crown presents some sign of unity. Not only should the material of a crown be weighed but its shape also offers grounds for attractive considerations. For the shape of a crown not only forms a continuous circle but also is somewhat elevated. Would you like an example of this clinging together and this single elevation? 'The believers', we read in Acts, 'had a single heart and a single soul.'* What is the purpose of this unity? It is surely 'for the hope which is stored up' for us among the heavenly.* Already then you have this continuous circle in unity and this elevation in hope. Again the apostle says: 'Don the helmet of salvation.'* Fittingly is mention made of a helmet, since it has some resemblance to a crown. Each is worn on the head, one as a protection, the other as an ornament. So there is nothing to prevent hope being related to each 'for in hope we were saved'.* Let these succinct remarks about the shape of the crown be sufficient. About its material, why do you ask? For you know yourselves that a lofty position scorns fragile and cheap material. It wants gold and precious stones. Indeed 'you have placed upon his head a crown of precious stones'.* Golden are the crowns of which you read in the Apocalypse.* The material is precious, whether it is solid gold or a mixture of gold and gems. But the psalm seems to suggest some greater measure of grace, because in omitting any mention of gold, the psalm claims: 'You have placed upon his head a crown of precious stones.'

Ac 4:32

Col 1:5

Eph 6:17

Rm 8:24

Ps 20:4
Rv 4:4

But I intend to show you a still more excellent material: 'A great sign appeared in heaven, a woman clothed with the sun . . . and upon her head a crown of twelve stars.'* Thus you are shown the choir of the apostles in their number and splendor, for 'those who instruct many' in wisdom 'shall shine like stars for ages unending'.* This crown of brothers stood in a circle around Jesus, as Luke wrote.* In the Apocalypse also are 'many diadems on the head' of the Bridegroom,* according to the diversity of graces and degrees. But one is pre-eminent, that with which he was crowned on his wedding day,* on the day on which he espoused the Church among his disciples. He espoused her in faith, he espoused her by setting in their hearts an earnest and a pledge and the first fruits of the Spirit.* An espousal is likewise called a sharing in the Spirit, when anyone clings to God and there exists not two 'but one spirit'.* In scriptural words, Christ also is the Man who left Father and mother to cling to his wife, and they became two in one flesh.* O blessed exchange! [O faithful soul], you were made with the bride in one flesh, and she was made with the Bridegroom in one spirit!¹⁰

9. How you ought to have rejoiced over such a wedding, faithful soul! How you ought to have rejoiced and kept high holiday!* Dress up, dress up in the robes of your glory, holy city,* bride of the Lamb; rejoice and be glad, O Sion united to Christ! How will you not rejoice while he himself rejoices? 'The Bridegroom will rejoice over the bride', says Isaiah, 'and your God will rejoice over you.'* But with how much joy? 'On the day of his bethrothal', says the Canticle, 'and on the day of the gladness of his heart.'* No slight emotion of gladness was intended, for the text mentioned the joy of his heart. Do I say gladness? It is sheer delight. 'My delights', we read in Proverbs, 'are to be with the children of men.'* How dearly those joys cost you, good Jesus! You do not win them free of cost, for you purchased them by suffering in your flesh. Therefore the Canticle attributes this gladness to the heart alone.

It is an' insult to the Bridegroom, if while he rejoices you do not applaud from your heart, do not congratulate him, and fail to rejoice with him. It is akin to disdain or scorn not to 'rejoice with one who rejoices'* particularly on the day of his wedding. Whose beauty will captivate your affection if not his who is 'handsome in form beyond the children of men'?* Rejoicing, rejoice in the Lord,* and let your soul exult in your Bridegroom, in your God; for if he were not God—but a man and nothing more—how many enticements to love would such a man yet have in himself, endowed with such abundance of graces? For if you begin to count his graces from the moment of conception, he will seem to you wholly decked with stars to the limit of man's lot, not only in the uniqueness but also in the excellence of his virtues, a man 'innocent, undefiled, set apart from sinners', not to mention for the moment that he 'became exalted above the heavens',* but that he is able 'to have compassion on our infirmities, was tried in all things as we are, except sin'.* Grace was poured out on his lips,* mercy in his heart, virtue in his hands;* he was without peer in his conduct, approachable in his talk; there was prudence in his answers,* life in his words. What of the fact that he was conceived by faith, born of a virgin, not swallowed up in death but taken up in glory?

Rm 12:15

Ps 44:3
Is 61:10

Heb 7:26

Heb 4:15
Lk 1:78
1 Ch 29:12
Lk 2:47

10. I say nothing now of the number of believers nor of the merits of the peoples whom he united with himself in faith and charity by sending the Spirit.* O surely Christ is the 'deep mystery of godliness', the goad of love; he was made visible and tortured in the flesh, justified in the spirit. He appeared to the angels, was proclaimed to the gentiles, believed in by the world and taken up into glory!* Who will grant me often to have discourse upon and recourse to these lines, and at each and every degree of his virtues and deeds to ask: 'Lord, who is like you?'* Who will grant that these words be written in my heart, cut with a stylus, engraved as it were on granite never to be effaced?* A good stylus is your finger, O Lord, the finger with which you wrote on the ground hidden words, words whose power accusers could not bear.* Bend down, my God, and carve on my heart the tables of your law.* Stony is my heart but

Lam 7, nn. 10, 13

1 Tm 3:16

Ps 34:10

Jb 19:23-24

Jn 8:6-9
Dt 10:1-4

hard rock forgets its nature at the impress of your finger, ready to yield where you engrave.

Now we have already spoken at length about the reason why the bride should rejoice and be glad on the wedding day of her Beloved, the day of his heart's gladness. There is great cause for rejoicing on this day, such as to surpass the limits of man's heart and affections. No extrinsic rejoicing need be introduced here; sufficient for the day is its own rejoicing. Gentle you are, O Lord, and your spirit, a loving spirit, has been sent upon us. By faith and love you join the souls of men to you with the affection of a Bridegroom and you rejoice over their conversion. Hard is the heart which robs itself of the grounds for this rejoicing, minimizes its occasions, lessens its reasons. O how shameless and ungrateful am I, if I do not love such a one, so free from corruption and moved by such compassion towards me, not subject to necessity and steadfast in loving-kindness. I will love you, sweet Lord, if not for myself, at least for yourself, that I may satisfy your desire, afford you grounds for delight, reasons for rejoicing on your wedding day, the day of the gladness of your heart.

NOTES ON SERMON TWENTY

1. The first four paragraphs seem to have been written for one individual; par. 8 has the singular address, *vis, habes, tibi,* along with the plural. Adaptation is evident in the first sentence of par. 1, in *vultis* and *videtis* of par. 4, while par. 5-7 have plurals of address. The text and treatment would be appropriate for nuns; confirmatory evidence from the text is ambiguous, for *si conclusae estis,* of par. 3 could be an apostrophe to the daughters of Sion, with an obvious allusion to women or to men in cloister. The *sic state, charissimi,* is not conclusive, since it is a scriptural quotation, and could include men and women. S 20 ends without the usual prayer and flows smoothly into S 21.

2. Reading *videndum* for *vivendum* with Migne, Paris, 9605, Troyes 419.

3. Possibly G. refers to Bernard of Clairvaux, whom in S 22:1, G. calls *eruditus et eloquens,* not unlike the preacher here who is *disertus et eruditus.* Cornelius à Lapide 8:27, quotes a *written* comment of Bernard on the verse G. is discussing, which would fit G.'s description without being the words Gilbert heard and quoted. G. quotes: *Male locatae videntur quae jubentur egredi.* Bernard wrote: *Egredimini de sensu carnis ad intellectum mentis, de servitude carnalis concupiscentiae ad libertatem spiritualis intelligentiae. Egredimini de terra vestra et de cognatione vestra et de domo patris vestri . . . (Sermo in epiphania Domini* SBOp 4:302)

4. See Bouton, 'Fiches Cistérciennes,' p. 239.

5. *diffinies,* Flor., Mab., mss. Paris 6905, Troyes 419; *definies,* Migne.

6. Reading *advertistis* with mss. Paris 9605, Troyes 419; Mab. and Migne: *advertisti;* see Lam 13, nn. 42-44.

7. See Bouton, 'Fiches Cisterciens,' pp. 239-40.

8. Leclercq, 'Otia Monastica' 93:48.

9. Leclercq, 'Otia Monastica,' 93:47 and 49, 119:25; Lam 10, n. 31; 17, n. 69; 175, n. 35; 176, n. 40.

10. *O beatum commercium! facta es cum sponsa in carne una, et ipsa cum sponso in uno spiritu,* Flor., Mab., Migne; for the first Adam becoming the first Eve, see S 14:5. G. does not express the vocative or nominative feminine subject of *facta es,* which in the trans. is added in square brackets: [O faithful soul]. This faithful soul includes the individual addressed, the crown of apostles, and the Church, and is found in the next sentence, the first of par. 9. Though the translator must take responsibility for this solution, I wish to acknowledge assistance from Martinus Cawley OCSO, F.E. Crowe SJ, and R. A. F, MacKenzie SJ, who steered me away from extravagant speculation.

SERMON 21
WONDER OVER HIS TWO NATURES

With wonder the bride contemplates the two natures in one Person. 1. Angels descend to marvel at the mysteries of the Incarnation. 2. We can imitate the angels in reverence for one who brings the good news. 3. Angels leave the wine-cellar of heaven to wonder at the inebriating chalice of the Incarnation, the union of two natures in one Person. 4. Be jubilant over his plenty; amazed at his prudence; enamored of his piety. 5. His Church adorns, encompasses, and crowns her Beloved. 6. There is one day of the espousals, the crowning, and the joy; in the heart of Christ is the place for daughters of Jerusalem.

GO FORTH, DAUGHTERS OF SION, AND BEHOLD KING SOLOMON IN THE DIADEM WITH WHICH HIS MOTHER CROWNED HIM ON THE DAY OF HIS BETROTHAL AND HIS JOYFULNESS OF HEART*[1]   *Sg:11*

You also, O daughters of the heavenly Sion, daughters of the Jerusalem which is in heaven, I make bold confidently to invite to rejoice at this vision. You are the true and full daughters of Sion, for you 'always gaze upon the face of the Father'.* You, I say, you hosts of many thousands of angels, you I invite and summon. 'Come forth and behold'; come forth from the hidden bosom of inmost vision, from the mystery of light   *Mt 18:10* inaccessible.* Our earth offers you a new spectacle, for the Lord has wrought something new upon earth. I am luring you from the eternal to the terrestrial. This invitation is a surprise, but somehow the eternal realities which in themselves are ever new and wonderful show a newer and more wonderful brilliance in the new reality wrought upon earth.²

O blessed is this revolution in time and space, which more fully renewed that ancient and eternal revolution revealed to angels! The Lord 'will bring about' something new upon earth: 'a woman will encompass a man'.* Who is this man? 'Behold a man', says Zechariah, 'whose name is the Day-Star.'* The Day-Star, the splendor of eternal light, is encompassed in the womb of a woman—yes, in a virginal womb—and clothed in flesh. This is that revolution which by the very excess of its novelty would now be beggaring belief, if faith had not previously been fostered by unprecedented signs. Amid so many manifest testimonies of prophecies and prodigies in Scripture, the wits of some have been so stunned by this new wonder that as long as they reject faith in this wonder they do not attune their belief to the most unimpeachable evidence.

But why do I invite you to come forth, you angels who everywhere anticipate and guide the apostles themselves? Everywhere you are eager to marvel at and proclaim this revolution.³ An angel announces to Mary the Lord's conception;* an angel announces his birth to the shepherds. Indeed not only to the shepherds but to the angels themselves an angel seems to have made the announcement. One proclaims, while the others applaud. 'There was with the angel', says Luke, 'a multitude of the heavenly host praising God and singing: Glory to God in the highest.'* One announces what the others knew equally well and yet they hear as something new and recent what could not be unknown to them. O blessed is this wonderful news which affords joy to the hearing of angels and which makes them delight in listening and, as it were, learning again from another what truth itself taught them from the

1 Tm 6:16

Jr 31:22
Zc 6:12

Lk 1:26-38

Lk 2:8-14

beginning! O humble and unwearied devotion, both towards God and towards one another!

2. Here is something and O! that we humans would behold it or rather hold it fast! What is it? That after the example of the angels we would lend a humble and attentive hearing to a stranger's account, even in matters where we are not ignorant. Not that he is a stranger who is from God, unless we consider ourselves strangers from God. Even if he is a stranger, his message from God invests him with authority. To have a distaste for what is known is a sign either of idle curiosity or of contumacy. The angelic spirits to whom the mystery of the Incarnation was made known from the beginning do not withhold their wonder at the revelation of this novelty, and their longstanding knowledge rejoices and is overjoyed not only at seeing but also at hearing the news. 'At the end of the ages'* Christ came forth; therefore they also come forth. His coming forth is also from the days of eternity.* But at the end of the ages, his coming forth is from the womb of the woman who encompassed him. Therefore the daughters of the heavenly Sion come forth, to marvel at the realization of what they always marvelled at in anticipation.

Dn 11:13

Mi 5:2

There was an angel at the annunciation,* an angel at the nativity,* an angel at the baptism.† An angel appeared to Christ as he prayed,* one was a witness of his resurrection† and stood by at his ascension.*⁴ What tremendous lovers, do you not agree, are such eager heralds and such indefatigable admirers! Through all the stages of this mystery they gather round and offer their homage of reverence, their homage of acclamation; they make melody and sing psalms to the Lord.* And all this veneration was openly displayed without a word about what is hidden within.* If the Lord wrought something new upon earth, still the fragrance of this wonderful news filled the heavens. 'A woman will encompass a man' as a crown encompasses the head. For 'the head of the Church is Christ'.* He is radiant indeed in the brilliance of God's glory and the impress of the

Lk 1:26-38
*Lk 2:9-14
†Lk 3:21
*Lk 22:43
†Lk 24:4
*Ac 1:10

Rv 5:11-12

Sg 4:1, 3

Eph 5:23

Father's substance,* but with the added dye, as it were, and the inlaid coloring of our nature; while he dims his own light, he increases the delight not only of those who otherwise could not bear his light but also of the angels on whom his splendor shines in its purity.

3. However, I suggest that this very condescension which led him to become incarnate seems to have brought some beauty to the dignity of his majesty. For what is more attractive than the lowliness of the Highest, the outpouring of Immensity, the Divine become incarnate? What is more beautiful than this exchange? Do I say exchange? It seems to be rather an exchange of opporsites, the more beautiful to contemplate, the more these opposites are not in conflict but in agreement with each other. Wonderful in itself is the divine Simplicity, but, if I may so express it, this new blending is much more wonderful because it is newer. I cannot marvel enough at the art of this union nor, I think, can the angels. Indeed they have greater reason to wonder, for to them the pure Simplicity of the divine nature made itself known with greater clarity. That Simplicity is pure beyond comparison and therefore makes this union more wonderful.

What is this union in which each nature preserves its integrity? For neither does the one pass into the other, nor from both does some third and new nature result. What is new is that they come together in one Person. The contemplation of each is a kind of wine cellar. The angelic spirits were introduced into the nectar-sweet cellar of eternal Majesty, or rather they were stored there from the first moment of their creation. Now at last 'at the end of the ages',* this cellar of ours upon earth ferments with must of a new kind. O plentiful stores, stores spilling over and bubbling over from cask to cask!* Come forth, daughters of Sion, from the cellar of nectar-pure wine to this must, which wisdom has blended in a new mixing bowl.* O inebriating chalice, how sparkling you are and therefore how inebriating in your splendor! The eternal stream poured into this new chalice is broached with greater charity though with temperate splendor, so that even love becomes intemperate. For who would make himself temperate in love, when immeasurable Majesty tempered itself to our capacity? O chalice, intoxicating the minds not only of men but also of angels and drawing angels away from the contemplation of undiluted Divinity to contemplate You in this new blending!

'Come forth, daughters of Sion', from that abundance of pure wine to this tempered chalice. Come forth and taste how sweet the Lord is.* Where you are, the simple nature of divine sweetness is envisioned; here the enjoyment and proofs of his sweetness are set before us. There he is seen in himself; here in his affection;⁵ in this latest birth, he and his affection are amazing and I know not which I marvel at more, the union of natures in one Person or the reason for this union. Why are we amazed any longer that there are three Persons in the unity of the divine Essence? Be amazed now that two natures exist in their integrity in one Person. What exists here that is not delicious to contemplate, that does not move our affections? *Ps 33:9; 1 P 2:3*

4. Then, to crown our wonder, comes its cause. It is a cause which does not lack the logical coherence of reason or the efficacy of salvation or the grace of compassion. Do you wish to hear what is the logical coherence? 'Just as all men die in Adam, so all men will be brought to life in Christ',* and again Paul says: 'Just as by one man's disobedience many were made sinners, so by one man's obedience many are made righteous.'* What is more logical? Great is the logical sequence, but here, considering justification, there is greater effectiveness; as Paul says: 'where sin abounded, grace abounded still more.'* Where sin existed, there temptation and deceit intervened; therefore the sin does not seem to be wholly deliberate. But in grace exists nothing which is not planned, nothing which is not deliberate. How then are good things which are deliberate not more efficacious than evils which are, as it were, partly coerced? Well assuredly grace is efficacious and *1 Co 15:22* *Rm 5:19* *Rm 5:20*

ingenious. I know not which to admire more, the ingenuity of adaptation or the efficacy of salvation. Each aspect of this gratuity is pleasing, both the will to save us and its effectiveness.

Add a third aspect too: the manner and plan. Nothing is more full of affection than this good will. What love is greater 'than to lay down one's life for one's friends'?* But this he did for enemies. They were not only enemies in themselves but also his friends, because he loved them before the creation of the world. What could be more fruitful than the harvest of his good work? The generous outpouring of the Spirit upon all flesh makes this sufficiently clear. The outpouring of the blood of Christ won for us an outpouring of the Spirit. Those whom he washed in his blood, how could he not flood with his holy Spirit? Hence he first washed them, that they might be the ones whom afterwards the Spirit might cleanse more deeply. In the logical order, what is more consistent? I am embarrassed in considering this mystery, because I know not which of three points I should especially select for contemplation: his piety, his prudence, or his plenty. These vie with one another for our attention, and while we lean towards one, we are tugged towards another. All three cajole and wheedle me with varying affections. I am enamored, amazed, jubilant; jubilant over his plenty; amazed at his prudence; enamored with the love his piety spent upon me.

5. Why do I divide up their roles? These three are mistaken for one another and in each there is frequent confusion. For the manner, the appositeness and the affection, or if you prefer other names, his prudence, his plenty, his piety, these three I say, whether considered simultaneously or singly, draw my spirit to themselves more quickly, captivate it longer, and turn it to a kind of wonder and exultation. From the variety of such virtues, the faith of Mother Church wove his diadem. These virtues determine the specific number, weight and measure of the diadem. In the logic and sequence of order is discerned the number and the measure of agreement; in weight, the more

Jo 15:13

powerful affection of piety. Truly powerful is the weight of grace, for it draws the immense Majesty from heaven to earth. This Immensity, incomparably surpassing all creation, confined itself to a limit, a limit which enabled it to reach downward even to us. For this Immensity did not simply extend itself further in our direction, as if it were not coming down to our level, but rather according to our measure it distills to us the gifts of the Spirit.

I understand a measure in the *efficacy* of these gifts. For not according to measure is God's *gift* of the Spirit[6] but in measure and against measure: in the measure of grace, against the measure of unrighteousness. For 'as sin abounded, so grace abounded still more'.* Or is measure here not against measure? Surely against and above. For 'grace abounded still more'. Was grace only above the measure of sin? No indeed, not only above the measure of sin but also above the measure of grace. Grace abounds both against and above the measure of unrighteousness, as grace abounds above the measure of grace but not against it. For where one abounds, the other also must necessarily abound still more, and more abundant gifts must be given to one who has in abundance. This measure is a 'good measure, pressed down and shaken together and spilling over'.* There seems to be a spilling over, when not only necessities are supplied but luxuries are multiplied. Among the gifts of the Spirit, some facilitate, some teach, some delight or heal or adorn or cheer. How do graces so plentiful not spill over?

But enough has now been said about the number, measure and weight of the diadem his mother fashioned for King Solomon. For she invests him as it were with a garland of glory, while she joins together the humanity he assumed from us and the divinity he revealed to us. You see in what a dowry of graces this diadem consists. But what connection has a diadem with graces? 'Wisdom will give to your head', says the Book of Proverbs, 'increases of graces'.* The Father gives and the mother crowns. She herself crowns, because she believes, because she

Rm 5:20

Lk 6:38

Pr 4:9

encompasses, because she crowns as a Mother. The Church, good Jesus, adorns you with herself, clothes you with herself, shoes you with herself,* and with herself makes a crown for your head. Her shoeing is for the journey, her crowning for journey's end. Here is a surprising metamorphosis, for after any accumulated dust has been shaken off, shoes are transformed into a crown!*

6. 'On the day of his betrothal and his joyfulness.' Notice the order. One and the same is the day of his betrothal and his crowning. If you recognize this, you are happy if you observe it.* You change the order, if you seek your betrothal before your crowning, if you would be bound to Christ for pleasure and repose before you conquer with Christ. Such is a felicitous but a disorderly anticipation, if you choose to have the bridal chamber furnished for you before your triumph, if you claim joy before toil. Only one day has been appointed for these three: the diadem, the betrothal, and the joyfulness of heart. And what is the heart of our Solomon? 'You are the body of Christ', says Paul, 'and individually its members.'* Happy indeed is any member with this head, but whoever is his heart is among the foremost members. Consider whether that person is not the heart who is cherished in the ventricle of God's secrets, in the vital warmth of his affections, in the center of his designs. For 'from the heart come forth designs', not actions.* Rightly then is he the heart who is set in the center of spiritual thoughts, in the richness of graces, in a kind of ventricle of truth, in the womb of wisdom whose symbol is Solomon. In effect, either the Church or an individual soul, but one and the same, is all three: crown and heart and bride; a crown upon his head, a bride from his side, the heart in his breast; the crown on top, the bride at his right hand, the heart within him. What here is not arranged to perfection? What is not in readiness for a wedding feast?

Go hence, our 'daughters of Sion, and behold', that you also may pass into the affection of his heart, into the grace of his bride, into the beauty of his diadem. Do not take pride in an empty name. Be what you are said to be, daughters of contemplation. Let your practice be a witness of your title. For the day of your betrothal is a feast day, one worthy to welcome God, and it reaches from our day to one more festive still, a wedding day, a day on which no writ of divorce is given, no separation intervenes, a day on which the Bridegroom does not depart on the longest journey nor even on the shortest, but on which the Bridegroom, Christ Jesus, remains evermore at home, for he lives and reigns with God the Father and the Holy Spirit for ever and ever. Amen.[7]

NOTES ON SERMON TWENTY-ONE

1.   No indication of G's audience occurs until *vide* and *adde* in par. 4, with *videtis* towards the end of par. 5; the first half of par. 6 is in the second person singular, the last third in the second person plural, addressed to *nostrae filiae Sion*. What was probably written by G. for one individual shows adaptation, perhaps for a final profession of nuns.
2.   Reading *et mirabiliora* with Mab., mss. Paris 6905, Troyes 419; Migne: *in mirabiliora*.
3.   Reading *et admiratores* with Mab., mss. Paris 6905, Troyes 419; Migne: *ad admiratores:* see Lam 251, n. 53.
4.   *astiterunt;* Mab, Migne, mss. Paris 6905, Troyes 419: *astat*.
5.   Reading *affectu* with Migne and Paris 6905; Mab., Troyes 419, Laon 59: *effectu*.
6.   I have underlined *efficacy* and *gift* to bring out G.'s distinction, and restored the negative to the text of Jo 3:34.
7.   Bernard frequently refers to the angels in his Sermons on the Canticle (SC 5, 7, 19, 27, 30, 31, 39, 41, and so on); cf. E. Boissard, 'La doctrine des anges chez S. Bernard,' *S. Bernard Theologien,* ASOC 9 (1953) 11-135, and 'S. Bernard et le Pseudo-Aréopagite', RTAM 26 (1959) 214-63. On angels, see the article by Joseph Durr, 'Anges' in DSp 1 (1936) 580-625, and on 'Cor et cordis affectus' see DSp 2 (1953) 2294, article by Jean Châtillon.

SERMON 22
THE EYES OF A DOVE

The Bride ascends to his vision and discerns what is good. 1. The Bridegroom increases his praise as the Canticle proceeds. 2. The bride has the eyes of doves in her purity of intention. 3. She avoids evil intentions in her own actions and a perverse interpretation in the actions of others; prudence of the flesh and of the spirit are incompatible. 4. She cannot judge herself or another because of the graces and gifts which lie hidden within. 5. The simplicity of a dove is a mystery within. 6. Virtues are divided into exterior, interior, and intimate. 7. Mysteries hidden from man should be treated with reverence.

HOW BEAUTIFUL YOU ARE, MY LOVE, HOW BEAUTIFUL! YOURS ARE THE EYES OF DOVES, APART FROM WHAT LIES HIDDEN WITHIN.*[1]   *Sg 4:1*

The Bridegroom is not afraid that she whose beauty he extols for himself so vividly will be puffed up with the gusts of his praises and jettison her humility. Beneath a great desire to please often lurks the fear of displeasing and too intense a devotion lessens and robs one's peace of conscience. What wonder is it, then, that the Bridegroom compliments her on her beauty and with flattering words calms her affections, which fear has troubled? For why should any human soul not fear its own ugliness, when it has been joined in marriage with our Solomon? The bride heard that in the depth of his glory he was more handsome than usual in his diadem, on the day of betrothal and of gladness of heart; so rightly she could fear rejection, if she looked to the cause of her ugliness and abjection. It was fitting then that, once reassured, she should take courage and that the alacrity of mind imparted to her should suffuse her features with a lively warmth. For cheerfulness of mind adds most to the fair countenance of all one's life and work.

Therefore the Bridegroom addresses his beloved in this way: 'How fair you are, my beloved!' Almost identical words were spoken above in earlier verses: 'Behold you are fair, my beloved, behold you are fair.'* There is little difference between 'Behold you are fair' and 'How fair you are'. In each, her beauty is extolled and the repetition only proves that the compliment is deserved. But to the best of my knowledge a slight distinction is here suggested. Where he says: 'Behold you are fair', he is concerned only with beauty, but here he alludes to its surpassing quality: 'How fair you are, my beloved, how fair!' in the former verse there is a simple recognition of beauty suddenly noticed, whereas here there is wonder at its surpassing quality. In the earlier verse he acknowledges how beautiful she is; here he rejoices that she is so beautiful. For this verse is pronounced with the greater conviction and passion of a mind surprised and the manner of speech betrays the emotion of a mind overjoyed: 'How fair you are, my beloved, how fair!' Indeed as the Canticle proceeds it is right that more perfect verses be sung to the bride. So much for my distinction between similar statements. But the required interpretation of the bride's beauty has been developed at length and with accuracy in the proper place. Whether the author is more remarkable for learning or for eloquence I know not, but the matter in the pages of his homilies it ill becomes me to turn over for discussion, pardon me, even with my little finger.[2]

2. This much, however, should be carefully observed, that after a general commendation of her

Sg 1:14

beauty, when the Bridegroom is about to sketch her individual features, he begins first with her eyes. Wisely indeed since 'if the eye be simple, the whole body will be full of light'.* Therefore he compares her eyes to those of doves so that, according to the teaching of the Gospel, he may show that 'his beloved is as simple as a dove'.* In fact, the simple eye of one's intention throws light on the whole body of one's work and insures that deeds which of themselves could shine before men would shine before God.* For when a good deed shines outwardly, but the spirit does not intend the goodness of the deed, it is like a blind eye in a body full of light. The deeds themselves are sometimes good of their kind and useful to others, but the goodness of the deeds does not reflect on the doer because he does not have a simple eye in performing them. They are deeds of darkness, because they lack the light of a pure intention. Good then is a simple eye, for it has no share of darkness and makes bright the whole body of man's behavior.

 The eye is either wholly dark or wholly light, or it has some admixture of darkness. It is wholly dark, when it intends an evil deed for the sake of evil; it is wholly light when it intends a good deed only for its goodness. But when, in a good deed, the intention is directed not only to the good but also to some other end, or when, in a deed that is not good, the good which was believed to be present is loved mistakenly, to some extent the eye is clouded and is not clear with unspoiled simplicity. What is to be said when a good deed is alleged and not that good but something entirely different is intended? Shall that eye be called wholly dark or to some extent clouded? To me it seems rather to be wholly dark. For even if some light is detected in the deed, still none is recognized in the intention. But how is an intention good which does not choose the good? Or how is it simple, when it hides itself under the cloak of good? In the eyes of the bride, however, both are commended, simplicity and spirituality. Therefore hers are called the eyes of doves. Appropriately, too, in

Mt 6:22-23.
Lam 195, n. 166.

Mt 10:16. See Morson, 162-3, White 144-5, on the dove.

Mt 5:16, Mk 1:10, Jo 1:32

his beloved does he first commend the light, that he may show her resemblance to himself, for he is himself called the light of the world,* and in him there is no darkness.* In the creative work of the six days, light is said to have been created first of all,* and when the bride's beauty is portrayed, mention of light is fittingly introduced in the first place.

3. 'Yours are the eyes of doves.' Why do you assume that you are the bride, when you know not how to possess the eyes of a dove? However good your deeds may have been, if your intention is not pure, you congratulate yourself in vain on your beauty. How are you beloved, when you are not beautiful? But how are you not an enemy, you who malign what is holy?* To malign what is holy is to malign what is good, whether it is one's own or that of another; you malign your own good when you do not see goodness itself, and you malign another's good when you entertain empty suspicions of that good. A wrong intention and an unfavorable interpretation—each is malicious, each is venomous, each false, having nothing in common with the nature of doves. The eyes of doves are those which neither wish to be deceived nor know how to deceive. Do you not know that your Bridegroom is Truth? How will he say to you: 'My dove, my beloved!'* when you do not rejoice in simplicity?³ Simplicity is the beloved of truth; therefore truth consorts with the simple.⁴ In our text, the Bridegroom praises the simplicity of his beloved with the words: 'Yours are the eyes of doves'. Wide-eyed simplicity is good, for it closes its eyes to pretence yet is not blind to the truth. The dove is a 'rare bird on earth'⁵ today and if anywhere it flocks together in numbers, it is well hidden, 'lurking in the clefts of the rock, in the nook of a wall' and 'above streams of water'.*

darkened! Who does not pursue the crafty ways of the world, who does not rejoice to profit from them who would not love to master them, or would not at least wish them to be attributed to himself? Who is not ashamed of dove-like eyes? Who does not boast of having the eyes of a kite?*⁶ If you wish to be called Christ's beloved, why do you act with 'the wisdom of the flesh which is hostile to God'?* Or why do you try to purge their animosities, that you may establish in yourself both the wisdom of the flesh and the wisdom of the spirit? 'A little yeast sours all the dough.'* What will happen then, when there is much yeast and little dough? What fellowship can there be between the law of covetousness and the law of charity? The former should not be associated with the latter, since greed cannot be subject to love.* For wisdom of the flesh is either opposed and hostile to the law of God or it perishes altogether and is nought; it either defies the law of God or it dies. It can be cut down, so that it ceases to exist altogether; it cannot be cut down to size, so as to yield to the law. You are choosing then to have both your lips and your heart practised in that kind of wisdom which can be neither associated with nor joined to the law of God. 'Wisdom of the spirit is life and peace.'* Wisdom of the spirit is alive, for it enjoys both the present life and the life to come. But wisdom of the flesh is operative only in the present life, destined to have no place in the life to come. For neither need nor use for covetousness exists in hell, but only crucifixion.[7] The one wisdom is peace, the other strife. And peace is to the point, for when wisdom becomes devoid of peace, wisdom becomes null and void. Such wisdom Christ links with the beauty of the bride. Such wisdom is portrayed in her dove-like eyes, for her wisdom reflects simplicity and spirituality, because in the figure of a dove the holy Spirit is usually understood.* Such simplicity is not wont to be empty, for much hidden grace lies concealed within.

Rm 8:7

1 Co 5:6

Rm 8:7

Rm 8:6

Mt 3:16, Mk 1:10, Lk 3:22, Jo 1:32

4. 'Yours are the eyes of doves, apart from what lies hidden within.' A great mystery is that, unquestionably great, which openly either should not be uttered or could not be uttered; nor could it be figuratively presented in a simile as other graces are, but it is left only to be guessed at or imagined by those who perhaps have similar experiences.[8] 'Apart from what lies hidden within', as if the other graces

and gifts of the Spirit were not within. And how is 'all the glory of the King's daughter from within'?* In our text, those dove-like eyes are within, where simplicity of faith purifies the heart and gives light to the eyes of the heart, where not only the eye but the whole inner self of the heart is said to be hidden.* But although all interior glory is from within as far as it is glory, and although just as in the outer self so in the inner self some things are more intimate than others, hidden more deeply and known to the Beloved alone, perhaps some things are unknown even to the bride herself and she is not fully aware of the gifts divinely conferred upon her. What does it matter, if their sublimity be hidden, provided her humility is preserved? Your mystery is for you, good Jesus, your mystery is for you, and you alone take your delight in the hidden gifts of the bride.* Why do you not give us some slight revelation of that hidden mystery? Why do you not present figuratively that hidden beauty in which you delight? You entice us all the more to seek it when you say that it lies hidden within; you provoke our curiosity all the more by shrouding so great a mystery in silence. By your silence you draw us all the more. 'How great is the extent of this sweetness', which you consider must be hidden, as long as you do not explain it!* Whatever it is, it lies hidden within; but from these hidden recesses breathes the sweetest fragrance. Somehow while I guess that it is wonderfully sweet, I already sense that it is wonderfully sweet; already the affections have weighed what the understanding cannot pierce. This is stored with the bride and sealed in her treasure chest; the Beloved alone may enter there and unroll the mysteries of her hidden glory.

5. This much however I do say, that it is not easy to define anyone's virtue from outward indications. For often when the colors one carries are ordinary, the mysteries within are extraordinary. Therefore we should so praise manifest virtues as to add after each this observation: 'apart from that which lies hidden within.' In our text, consider this dove-like simplicity commended in the bride and of

which we are speaking. How gratifying, how gentle and agreeable it is in itself; yet it has greater treasures stored within and, so to speak, its very marrow contains a gentle secret. Do you ask what that is? I have already confessed, and if you wish to hear it a second time, I confess that I do nòt know. I could recommend this devout simplicity to you and exhort you to emulate it, because it contains and perhaps bestows so inexplicable and gentle a mystery. But if I try to unravel the mystery either by experience or by conjecture, I might perhaps reach something hidden and concealed. But will that be what the Bridegroom mentions in so involved a way in his praise of his beloved? No matter what hidden treasure I shall be able to dig out, something will still lie buried within. It lies hidden in deep darkness and is not accessible either to our pen or to our pursuit. I shall respect the very silence of so great a mystery. For although it has not been granted to know precisely what it is because it is cloaked in silence, there is evidence enough to believe it is something exceptionally gentle and pleasing to the Bridegroom. Though its nature cannot be traced, its greatness can be guessed, if only from the fact that it was not permitted to utter a word so hidden.

6. However, that I may seem to have spoken some word and not to have been wholly silent—for you insist on this—listen to what I think can be said without contradiction on this subject; whether it fits our text is for you to judge. Virtues by their very nature are located interiorly in the spirit, but in practice some are directed towards outward things, whereas some exercise their power interiorly. The nature of the former virtues resists the lures of the flesh, while the nature of the latter embraces the secrets of spiritual delights. The former nature either flies from occasions of temptation or represses wanton affection and must toil at a journeyman's job which, however necessary for the present, is none the less irritating; the latter enjoys an occupation which offers not only greater reward but also greater distinction. While the former scans outward ap-

pearances with simple gaze and dove-like eye, it is filled with loathing or scorn; the latter with more searching gaze ranges through heavenly appearances to catch more fire from these horizons. So we can formulate some such distinction and say that some virtues are outward, others more inward, others inmost. For some withdraw themselves from things of the flesh, others attend to things spiritual, while others already attain some firstfruits. The first restrain themselves from the world's charm which they scorn; the second are still composing themselves for what they spiritually desire; the last, or rather the inmost, already enjoy what they eagerly desired. O God of goodness, what light and delight exist in those hidden recesses, what transport in those inward depths! Would that such recesses might enclose me, that I might sing the verse of the psalm: 'This night is my illumination in my delights.'*

Ps 138:11

7. Look, now I have touched upon something hidden at this last step and perhaps it is this or something similar which the Bridegroom intended. For the rest I wish to bow before mysteries; for it is not right in a glib talk* to lay bare the secrets of prayer and with the unhallowed hands of the tongue to unroll the delicately wrapped scrolls of the Holy of holies and to handle the hidden manna, stored in the golden urn, in the Ark, in the Holy of holies, that the inquisitive and less worthy eye may be kept from such a vision,[9] the eye which knows not how to be dove-what it is. And to what rather than to manna shall I compare our secret? Manna is a sweet food from heaven, but you see how secretly it is hidden in the urn, in the Ark, in the Holy of holies, that the inquisitive and less worthy eye may be kept from such a vision,[8] the eye which knows not how to be dove-like, which is not directed by devout belief and pure intention. However we invite you, brethren: embrace holy simplicity, repose of mind, pure meditations, free prayer, for in such vessels and so to speak, in the ark of holy meditation and in the interior urn of prayer,[10] there is set for us a divine nourishment and that portion of glory of which we read: 'I shall be

Si 21:8

2 M 5:16. Lam 172, n. 15

filled when your glory appears.'* May its plenitude   *Ps 16:15*
confer upon us eternal life, through Jesus Christ, to
whom is honor and glory for ever and ever. Amen.

NOTES ON SERMON TWENTY-TWO

1. In par. 3, a long apostrophe in the second person singular, addresses the Synagogue rather than an individual; the last three paragraphs are in the plural, to his brethren probably: *quaeritis . . . vultis . . . vobis . . . vos,* par. 5; *vos videritis,* par. 6; *vos fratres,* par. 7.
2. Bernard, SC 40, noted by Mab., specifically SC 40:4, and 45:1-3, 6; see also William of St Thierry, Cant. S 1, St. 8:90, CF 6 (1970) 73-74.
3. Mab: *quae simplicitate non gaudes?* The clause is omitted by Migne.
4. Pr 3:32. See Jean Leclercq, 'The Monastic Tradition of Culture and Studies', ABR 11 (1960) 121-129, on simplicity of heart.
5. Juvenal, 6:164; in his 'Legend of bad women', Juvenal speaks of a good woman, *rara avis in terris,* a rare bird on earth, rare but real like a black swan. Bernard (*In circumcisione domini* SBOp 4:291:7) says of discretion: *omnino rara ista avis est in terris.* For the popularity of Juvenal in the Middle Ages, see *Friedlander's Essays on Juvenal,* trans. John R. C. Martyn (Amsterdam: Hakkert, 1969) 54-57.
6. The kite, *milvus,* a thief; see White, p. 103.
7. Lk 16:24; Mab, mss Paris 9605, Troyes 419: *opus*; Migne, *opes.*
8. See Miquel, p. 154.
9. Reading *ab hujusmodi aspectu* with Mab, mss Paris 9605, Troyes 419; Migne: *aspectus.* Lam 84, n. 2.
10. See Leclercq, 'Otia Monastica', 112:53; for meditation and prayer as a pair, see Lam 185, nn. 95, 101.

SERMON 23
DISCERNMENT IN WISDOM

The bride ascends to His Wisdom and discerns what is good. 1. As the eyes of the Church are prophets, apostles, interpreters, teachers, however blind some moderns may be, so her locks are the flocks of disciples. 2. The locks of the Church cling to the head, which is a mount of witness. 3. The daily life of the Cistercians is a white martyrdom, a mount of witness to Christ. 4. A religious without fruit is condemned by the fruit of those rooted in Christ. 5. The cairns of witness of the martyrs and saints encourage our cowardice. 6. The teeth of the Church are prelates who crop the vices of others, though some others bite back. 7. Prelates also break crusts for the weak, and must be clean and without reproach. 8. Be washed here in a pool of water rather than there in a pool of fire; here let our chief business be meditation, for there our only business will be contemplation.

YOUR HAIR IS LIKE A FLOCK OF GOATS THAT HAVE COME UP FROM MOUNT GILEAD. YOUR TEETH ARE LIKE A FLOCK OF SHORN EWES THAT HAVE COME UP FROM THE WASHING*[1]   *Sg 4:12*

These compliments, as you well know, are meant for the Church. The previous sermon discussed her spiritual eyes. But since her eyes are spiritual, are they also rare? See how her whole body 'front and back is full of eyes'.* Her eyes are the prophets, her eyes are the apostles, for they either foresee the future or proclaim the past. Her eyes are the interpreters of prophets and apostles and the teachers of the peoples; thanks to their ministry, we see and discern both the spiritual aids and the stumbling-blocks of the soul.

But I know not whether all who hold the ministry of the eye make good use of it. Blind leaders not only of the blind* but also and more unworthily of those who have eyes, do they not seem to possess the position and the beauty of the eye but to lack its power? Would that this lack were their only fault, that they lacked the power of providing good things and were blind to common gains, if only they were not crafty for private profit. As it is, they are both blind and cunning: blear-eyed toward the gains of the Church, sharp-eyed toward their own gain. How is he the eye of a dove, who does not serve the dove, does not see for the dove, does not provide for the dove, who does not lead but rather misleads the dove, the Church, and so far as lies in him ensnares her by bad example? Of such Paul says: 'All seek their own interests, not those of Jesus Christ.'* Such men occupy a position and subvert it in practice. On the contrary, others who do not hold the position of the eye by promotion, usurp it by presumption. Their number is legion. Among the number of disciples at this moment, in your opinion, who does not in his own judgement, as if presiding over a tribunal, criticize, correct and chastise the actions of superiors? Such fellows are no longer the eyes of the members but the eyes of the eyes, as if the wings and feathers on the body of a dove should wish to guide the line of vision of its eyes.*

I do not wish to press the point overmuch, brethren, lest I should seem to be disturbing you. Be content with your lot.* In the dove's body nothing whatever lacks its function, nothing lacks honor, and whichever members are hidden possess the greatest honor. In our text, even the locks of the bride have their own honor. For if her eyes are her prelates, what are meant by her locks but her disciples? Good indeed are her disciples, if like her locks they show themselves manageable, compliant to every nod of their master as to a gust of wind, graceful and refined by spiritual exercises,* almost without body and utterly without flesh, so insensitive to every insult that they do not feel the snip of a barber's scissors!² They endure the pangs of suffering only if they are plucked from the head to which they belong; for, dead to pain in the rest of their body, they retain vital sensation only at the point at which they are joined to the head from which they grow. Because they are close to the brain, where wisdom is said to have its abode, they strive, as it were, to enter into its inmost secrets. To be summoned to external cares on whatever pretext is for them to be pulled out of the head, as it were, by the very roots. As for those which drop from the head without any feeling of pain, how can they be supposed to have been born or rooted there?

Lam 171, n. 3

2. To see in the text that the bride's hair does not drop out but grows out, hear what follows: 'Your hair is like a flock of goats that have come up from Mount Gilead.' 'Like a flock of goats' sent out to pasture on a high plateau, they are always clambering up like goats,³ with no taste for lofty thoughts but aware of the weakness of the flesh.* For pride falls of itself; humility rises.* Therefore [they are] 'like goats' because they always seek the heights, while keeping an eye on their infirmities. And rightly do they 'ascend from Mount Gilead' and only on 'Mount Gilead', for it means the 'Mound of Witness'. And who is that but Christ, upon whom all the testimonies of the prophets have been piled, for to him the Prophets and John and the Father and his own works bear witness?⁴ This mount is the head of the Church.

Rm 11:20
RB 6:6-7

Do not fall from this mount, if you are a hair. Why do you threaten to be separated from us and to be plucked from the flock of the remaining locks? Will your fall inflict baldness on the Church? She cannot suffer baldness, for her hairs are all numbered.* It was to the Synagogue that the threat was made by Isaiah: 'Instead of curled locks there will be baldness.'* The locks of the Church are curled, always recoiling to her head, encircling it in friendly embrace, striving to enter the secrets of her head. Therefore her hairs do not tumble from but ascend from Mount Gilead, accumulating for their own imitation ever greater examples of Christ's works.⁵

Would that all my works might bear witness to the faith which I have in Christ* and, heaped up by constant progress, might build for me a mound of ascent. How few stones of this witness I have assembled for myself!* I fear indeed that I have even gathered many for the opposite purpose. For consider: do they not seem to you to have gathered evidence not for the faith but against the faith, those whose lives are such that they seem to belong to some faith other than the christian? How many do we see of whom it can rightly be said: these do not conduct themselves as men who believe they were redeemed by the blood of Christ, who hope for another life, who fear the judgement to come, and who profess that the precepts of the Gospel were at last given by God? May but few such testimonies be discovered near me; I would prefer that there were none, lest a little leaven spoil the whole mound of faithful works.*

3. Well, brothers, to boast a little of the common store, since I cannot boast of my private store, if you regard the order of your whole life and the round of regular observance,* you will see that the mound of good witness which you are building together is not negligible. For starting with nocturnal vigils, which with unwearying affection you savor as the first-fruits, if from the beginning of the night watches you pour out your hearts like water in the sight of God,* if, I say, you should wish to review in sequence from the beginning the steps of your divine way of life, what will you find there which does not speak of discipline, is not in harmony with our faith, does not either chasten the body or elevate the mind or guide the

the mind once elevated?* At psalmody, how great is the discipline of the body! How much greater is the discipline of the mind, in some who do not allow the mind to stray in the slightest way, or only in the slightest way, from the meaning of the words! For they either keep the mind tied to the very words of the chant or release it for related but never for alien themes. If the mind should stray—for the human mind is prone to wander—with what a reproach they at once correct it and exact of themselves a penalty for this delay.

Lam 170, nn. 2, 3; 171, n. 7; 187 n. 111.

But not even the intervals at night between the hours of common prayer are unoccupied. O God of goodness, how unlike night is that hour of the night, how that night is an illumination in delights!* Those prayers are made in private but they make petition for nothing private. The voice is indeed more subdued but the mind is more intent and silent prayers are full of inspiration. Often indeed passionate prayer* outstrips the voice; it neither needs nor uses words, for it is borne on the wings of pure and full affection. Love alone, beating on the ears of the Lord, disdains the sound of articulate words, which though they spur the beginner only impede one whose prayer is perfect. What follows after? At the morning hours they take up their prayers afresh, they flock to confession, and with modest but open disclosure they wash away even the slightest faults.* Not that they think it a slight fault, if they waver from Christ in the least remembrance. Any possible suggestion from the malice of their wily foe they charge against themselves like judges biased against themselves, while they consider it a fault of their own, though they were only troubled by the vain effort of another's deceit.

Ps 138:11. Lam 172, nn. 11, 12.

Lam 191, nn. 136, 140

Lam 193, n. 156

What of the daily manual labor, by which the body is both sufficiently exercised and frugally fed? Not they alone eat from their manual labor, but from their slender reserve they share with the needy, that they also may experience distress, provided others have plenty. At some intervals they lighten their toil, but in a weary body their affection is fervent. There silent tears flow copiously, lament is heard, sighs break forth, so that if perhaps those who sit near are cold themselves, they may catch fire from the sparks of their neighbors.* What of their heeding the Lord when they take no thought for tomorrow nor even for today, but cast all their care on the person in charge of them, seeking no reward but the kingdom of God? Now I had almost forgotten the daily chapter; every single day they submit to the judgement of the abbot for examination, as if brought before Christ's tribunal.* There each one is his own principal prosecutor, hastening to snatch from others the opportunity of self-accusation.

What of their continual silence and their gravity of demeanor? Does it not lend charm to their whole way of life and clothe it, as it were, with the fair features of holiness?* Sleep itself bears witness to holiness, nor does it fail to add its exhibit to such a pile of evidence. For echoes of thought confess to Christ when the body is submerged in sleep. How can vivid phantasms of the whole day's proceedings fail to flit before the eyes of the sleeper and keep watch in his spirit?

4. Does it not seem to you that a great cairn rather than a pile of evidence is raised here, for these stones are not heaped indiscriminately but each is placed in a fixed order and in its own good time. Has this evidence not become all too trustworthy, because 'such holiness befits your house, O Lord'?* Would that the roots of my heart might grow thick over this cairn. The high mount of such a good life cannot be barren. The site is high and fertile, such as the prophet describes: 'My Beloved had a vineyard on a fertile hillside.'* Clearly a more plentiful yield of fruit is good evidence of fertile soil, just as the richness of the soil shows the poor quality of a tree when, contrariwise, the tree lacks fruit. Or is that tree not worthless which, occupying good soil, produces no satisfactory fruits, does not even produce any blossoms of great expectation? Perhaps that barren figtree which the Lord ordered to be cut down,* was condemned by the fertile vineyards close

at hand. It is iniquitous for someone planted in a holy way of life not to produce something holy and, alleging excuses, to be disheartened by others' example and to plan in his heart a descent from the place whence others ascend. Let your own descent be enough for you, if such is your character. Why try to pull down the cairn of good deeds which others climb with eagerness? Why try to change the regular observances, complaining both of their number and of their strictness?* Do not hamper those who are doing well; if you can, climb up yourself. *Lam 170, n. 5; 195, n. 165.*

Learn of the height and slope of the mount from which the saints ascended: The saints 'suffered mockery and stripes and even chains and imprisonment. They breathed their last, slain by the sword. They went about in sheepskin and goats' hide, destitute, afflicted, ill-treated, wandering over deserts and mountains, and in dens and caves of the earth; and all these were tried by the witness of faith'.* Do you see with what torture their faith was tested, with what evidence it was tried? Is anything of the sort either asked or looked for from you? Yet your acts of witness here, of a lesser kind, are trustworthy enough, all the more trustworthy since they were not commandeered by necessity but volunteered by free will. Let free will then be free will, and let it rely on the right of its first freedom; let it show itself free to progress, not regard itself free to regress. Let it recognize a debt to necessity without feeling its yoke. Let it be free in good, and none the less free for good, both the goodness at hand and the goodness ahead; but in what lies behind, let it consider that no liberty is allowed.* *Heb 11:36-39 Lam 198, n. 181*

Ph 3:13

Finally hear from what a mount of witness Paul ascended: 'The Spirit himself bears witness to our spirit that we are children of God.'* What a mount in this one witness! But did He never bear witness outwardly? 'God bore witness by signs and wonders', says Paul, 'and various miracles, and by gifts of the holy Spirit distributed according to his own will.'* Though founded on so great a memorial of virtues and attesting graces, Paul admits: 'I do not claim that I have

Rm 8:16

Heb 2:4

the mastery already; but I do one thing: forgetting what lies behind I strain forward to what lies ahead.'* 'Let us also then, since we are surrounded by such a cloud of witnesses, lay aside every weight and the sin entangling us, and let us run with patience the race set before us, looking to Jesus the author and rewarder of faith, who for the joy set before him endured the cross, despising the shame, and is enthroned at the right hand of God. Consider him who endured from sinners such hostility against himself, that you may not grow weary or lose heart. For you have not yet resisted even unto blood.'* For the witness of those who shed their blood for the faith of Christ is called witness in a privileged sense, that is martyrdom. Consider first from what a mound of stones the first martyr Stephen ascended to Christ, Whom all righteous souls also follow.*

Ph 3:13

Heb 12:1-4

Ac 7:58; Ac 22:20

'Like a flock of goats', says our text, 'that have come up from Mount Gilead.' They carried the treasure of faith in vessels of clay, but the loftiness of their courage was from God.* So they are described as ascending, because savage tortures did not so much break them as strengthen them to bear witness with great courage. What spirit have these men on earth, who cannot endure a single rebuke on the part of their superiors, however light and friendly, but at one rather severe word all the self-assured firmness of their good resolution melts away? Their witness, supported by so many trellises, can hardly stand upright, and yet the martyrs' witness, assailed by so many tortures, blossomed the more abundantly. Did not every new torture but add to the total of their testimony? Although they were threatened with death the livelong day and reckoned as sheep for the slaughter,* in everything they conquered and, as it were, ascended on high from Gilead, from the mount of martyrdom. For the saints entered a contest to save not the life of the body but the life of faith by which the just man lives.*[6] Therefore they conquer in all things, for their cause stands firm. For how do they not conquer, when either by perseverance in the confession

2 Co 4:7

Ps 43:22

Rm 1:17

of faith they have been promoted to eternity, or by persuasion have prepared their persecutors for the truth? Although, as Scripture says, 'reckoned as sheep for the slaughter', with harmless teeth, as it were, they cropped their enemies from the root of unbelief to store them in the living bowels of the Church.

6. Is this not the meaning of what follows? 'Your teeth', says the text, 'are like a flock of shorn ewes.' You notice what sort of ewes these are:[7] they can indeed be shorn but their teeth cannot be ground down. They can be slaughtered but cannot be swayed. Or rather like teeth they broke their persecutors like crusts and, having softened them with words of unconquerable teaching, as if chewing them with their teeth, they passed them into the unity of the faithful.* Peter was told: 'Kill and eat.'* Even the teeth of Moses did not decay.* For their teeth are weapons and arrows: spiritual weapons powerful in God to demolish fortifications.* Or are the teeth of the Church not they of whom the apostle says: 'If an unbeliever or outsider should enter, he is convicted by all, he is called to account by all, the secrets of his heart are disclosed, and so, falling on his face, he will worship God and declare that God is really among you.'*

Sg 7:9
Ac 10:13
Dt 34:7

2 Co 10:14;
Ps 56:5

1 Co 14:24-5

Do not be afraid, brothers, of a bite from their teeth; they are not a hound's teeth but a sheep's teeth, for they are compared to a flock of shorn ewes. In hounds one prizes not the bite but the bark.[8] 'Silent hounds', says Isaiah, 'unable to bark, they never have enough to eat'*—as if Isaiah were upbraiding some watchmen first for shirking the duty of a watchdog to bay, and then for being as hungry as hounds; unable to bark, they cease not to bite. Such are backbiters, detractors, calumniators. Would that even so they were satisfied with biting and devouring one another, and did not try to bite the very teeth of the shorn ewes.[9] Does it not seem to you that her teachers and prelates are the teeth of the Church, for as if by the nibbling of kindly reproof, they check, discern, expose and mellow their subjects for a better

Is 56:10

state of life? But if you are obdurate and cannot be mellowed, why do you prepare to bite back? Or do you not bite back, when you either speak evil in secret or openly contradict? Why do you sharpen tooth against tooth, a wicked tooth against a loyal tooth? You can bite but you cannot devour. For teachers and prelates are teeth, and they are both hardy and firm; they do not fear detractors, remembering with the prophet that they dwell among scorpions[10] and unbelievers* and that they are sent like sheep among wolves* to change wolves[11] into sheep by reasonable tolerance and exhortation.* Aptly are they called the teeth of 'shorn ewes', because their bites should not be avoided, since for their subjects they give the example of good works like shorn fleece.

Ezk 2:6
Mt 10:6
2 Co 1:6

7. Yet teeth are considered useful not only for cropping and checking the errors of others. They have another more valuable use, if any are ready to masticate the solid bread of heavenly food and to distinguish and discern the hidden meaning of more sublime teaching, if any no longer need milk but solid food and can somehow break and soften it and by some seasoning either of exposition or of discussion make it suitable for those who of themselves are not ready for solid food and could assimilate only milk. For they have, as it were, dentures for masticating more solid food, since they have faculties skilled in the discernment of good from evil and indeed even of one good from another, not only judging between night and day but judging each and every day.* Aptly too the text says they come up 'from the washing', to prove them eager to cleanse the heart, inasmuch as the knowledge of God has been promised to the clean of heart.* You see how those who have to crop and check the excesses of others must be washed and irreproachable, how they must be washed and clean of heart, who have to dispense the nourishment of God's word and shake out the hidden meanings of the more mysterious utterances, and who must explore the inmost truths of wisdom and digest its inner substance.[12]

Rm 14:5

Mt 5:8

8. 'Your teeth are like a flock of shorn ewes.' Why then like a flock? Assuredly because the teeth of the Church do not butt and attack one another but show harmony and concord in simplicity and unity of spirit. 'Like a flock of shorn ewes that have come up from the washing.' For putting off the old self,* and relieved and cleansed of a superfluous burden, they climb the more eagerly to the heights. Surely the old hair begins to be a burden when the new fleece first emerges, when the winter has passed and the rains are over and gone.* Therefore if you still consider it necessary to be wrapped in the old and superfluous fleece of trivialities and vanities, for you the winter frosts of a frozen mind have not yet passed away. Appropriately therefore they have been shorn and go up from the washing, as if having nothing of the old burden or the mire.

Ep 4:22

Sg 2:11

Do you notice that it is not enough for you to be shorn, to be unburdened, to become washed and new, unless you immediately rise and progress in spirit, for you are renewed in spirit?* 'If we live by the spirit', says Paul, 'let us also walk in the spirit.'* If then you intend to rise, rise always from the washing ever new and clean. Each and every night wash your bed with tears.* Or if sin does not wrap you round like night but flies by like a cloud, none the less wash each and every night, blot out with your tears the traces even of slight sins. For here in the valley of tears is the place for washing. Why gather dust, why put off the cleansing of sin until the washing of the world to come? How do you know that a pool of fire will not exist there rather than a pool of water? For what could easily be washed out here, there is purified in a spirit not so much of mercy as of judgement and fire.

Ep 4:23
Ga 5:25

*Lam 193, n. 155;
194, n. 159.*

Happy is one who goes up from this world not as if from the mire but as if from the washing, with no need to wash a single thing in himself for 'he is wholly clean'.* Obviously he will be found worthy to eat the bread of angels with the glistening teeth of his soul's faculties, no longer the crust of grief but the bread which gladdens the heart of man,* that

Jo 13:10

*Ps 126:2; Pr 27:11.
Lam 172, n. 15.*

bread which the prophet meant when he said: 'I shall be filled when your glory appears.'* Just so your glory nourishes while it does not appear, but refreshes when it is revealed. Now what is the full revelation of this glory but true wisdom? When wisdom invites us to banquet upon itself, wisdom is digested by us only when we meditate on wisdom as the life-giving delight and unfailing refreshment of a pure mind. Here then let us keep the faculties of our spirit purified and schooled, not now to distinguish good from evil but only to perceive goodness so great. Here let us often practise what there we shall do without interruption; let us frequently anticipate what shall occupy us unceasingly. Here let this be our chief business, which there will be our sole business. For the contemplation of wisdom is eternal refreshment. Nothing whatever is ruminated with more savor by the spiritual teeth of the soul than that living Bread who says to the Father: 'This is eternal life, that they should know you, the true God, and Jesus Christ whom you have sent',* who lives and reigns, God for ever and ever. Amen.

NOTES ON SERMON TWENTY-THREE

1. G. addresses one person with some exceptions: e.g., *Nostis* and *vos, fratres,* in par. 1; *fratres mei . . . vestrae,* in par. 3; *audite* and *videte* in par. 5; *fratres* in par. 6.
2. G. seems to intend a wry reference to abstinence and tonsure.
3. For goats, see Morson, 161, White, 40-43.
4. Pauphilet, in *Etudes sur la 'Queste del Saint Graal'* (Paris, 1921) 135-8, showed that, according to Gn 36:47-52, 'Galaad meant "heap of testimony', and that Isidore of Seville, Walafrid Strabo and the Venerable Bede construed this etymology as a reference to Christ. He clinched the matter by quoting from a Cistercian work, the "Sermons on the Canticles" of Gilbert of Holland'. R. S. Loomis, *The Grail, from Celtic Myth to Christian Symbol* (N.Y.: Columbia U. Press, 1963) p. 179.
5. 'Here, then, the Synagogue or the Old Law is imagined as a bald woman, and the Church or the New Law as a woman adorned with luxuriant tresses. It is next to certain that this passage inspired the author of Perlesvaus.' R. S. Loomis, *The Grail,* 106-7. On the imitation of Christ in St Bernard, see A. Van Den Bosch, 'Le Christ, Dieu devenu imitable d'après S. Bernard', COCR 22 (1960) 341-355.
6. See Roger of Byland, *Lac Parvulorum,* R 18 below, Roger's vocation letter to G.
7. For sheep, see White 72-74.
8. For hounds, see Morson, 153, White, 61-8.
9. Mss Paris 9605, Troyes 419: *temptent;* Mab: *tenent;* Migne: *tentent.*
10. For the scorpion, see White, 192.
11. For the wolf, see Morson, 153, White, 56-61.
12. Perhaps an allusion to the vulture in the Prometheus myth. Lam 179, n. 55; 182-3, n. 76.

SERMON 24
UNDERSTANDING AND AFFECTION

The bride bears twins, the light of understanding and the warmth of affection. 1. The teeth of the bride help her understand and digest the Scriptures. 2. But she bears twins, both understanding and affection. 3. Her lips are like charity, for they wound, they bind, they are scarlet. 4. Such lips are praised for prayer ånd exhortation. 5. The tongue can enkindle a flame of hate or of love.

EACH ONE BEARS TWINS AND AMONG THEM NOT ONE IS BARREN. YOUR LIPS ARE LIKE A SCARLET RIBBON AND YOUR SPEECH IS ENCHANTING.*[1]   *Sg 4:2-3*

I n the previous sermon you heard praise for the teeth of the bride. And rightly, for no small measure of beauty is attributed to teeth if they are white and evenly matched. Not only is evenness pleasing in teeth but also usefulness. What is the reason? How was John to devour the rolled-up scroll proffered him by the angel in the Apocalypse,*   *Rv 10:9-11* without teeth fit for such food? An entire book seemed to be tough food and therefore teeth were needed to break the whole into small pieces and to soften what was hard that it might be swallowed more easily. Surely a good tooth is a trained understanding which is spiritual, which judges everything, examines everything, chews on and 'scrutinizes everything, even the abyss of God',* which chews even the very marrow   *Sg 7:9; 1 Co 2:10*

297

of the rolled up scroll and consumes the vitals of wisdom.* 'The fool,' we read, 'folds his hands and consumes his own vitals.'* That is gory food, carnal food, food which perishes, or rather which destroys. How much more appetizing and healthful [it is] to consume the vitals of wisdom and the mysteries of the sacred word. The word cannot be touched with gory teeth but only with teeth washed and white, because it is the 'brightness of eternal light'* and the teeth of the Bridegroom himself are called 'whiter than milk'.* Accordingly he praises in the bride teeth like his own. 'Your teeth are like a flock of shorn ewes which have come up from the washing'.* Anyone must have mental faculties not only washed but also freed, who intends them to scrutinize the word of God.

Ezk 3:3
Qo 4:5

Ws 7:26

Gn 49:12

Sg 4:1

2. 'Each bears twins and not one among them is barren.' Barrenness is attributed to you, if you are content with even a single offspring. If you have been able to arrive at some holy understanding in the Scriptures, you have already given birth to one offspring. This is a good, a giant step, but not enough for a holy appreciation, if affection does not match it. Barren is that understanding which is not paired with a contemporary and kindred devotion. Everywhere in the Scriptures, seed is sown for you, as it were, from which you may conceive this twin offspring. There all things are not only subtle but also sweet. The command of the Lord is full of light and his word full of fire.* Sterile in you is the word of God, so far as it fails to produce either light or fire. If you see with your understanding but are still chilled with icy feelings, is not the flaming power of God's word considered barren and ineffective in you?

Ps 18:9; Ps 118: 140. Lam 181, n. 68

In Scripture the word is called fire, not only because it gives light but especially because it ignites. 'The word which goes forth from my mouth,' says the Lord, 'shall not return to me empty but shall act . . . and achieve the end for which I sent it.'* What is this end? You have it in the Gospel: 'I came to cast fire upon the earth, and would that it were already kindled.'* A seed is the word of God and in

Is 55:11

Lk 12:49

it, as you read in Job, both light and heat are sown over the earth.* But somehow light has blossomed more bountifully and men have loved light more than the warmth of fervor, save that they may take more pleasure in light, without embracing the very source of the light. Or does it not seem to you that fire which does not kindle has lost or unlearnt its own nature? When you hear someone say boastfully: 'those words of sacred Scripture do not edify me', what else does that person seem to you to be saying but that 'the flaming Word has lost its effect upon me; it neither enkindles, nor inflames, nor exerts upon me any generative power'. His own sterility he imputes to the word, which for its part grows and bears fruit. What a glorious boast, brother, that the word of God does not edify you, because you say so! Perhaps the old sod in you has not been plowed and harrowed and therefore a new crop cannot be laid on top, cannot germinate, cannot sprout.

Jb 38:24

Happy the man in whom the sap of worldly love is dried up and its strength enfeebled; in him the power of the flaming word does its work easily. The word of God gives both light and warmth. Let neither be robbed of its power in you. Conceive a twin offspring from this seed. Barren is the womb considered which is not pregnant with these twins. 'In Christ Jesus neither circumcision has any value, nor has uncircumcision, but only the faith which works through love.'* Love is indeed a good offspring, since charity is listed among the fruits of the Spirit. In Scripture, the twin offspring are like our twofold charity. 'You shall love the Lord your God with your whole heart and your whole soul and your whole mind. This is the greatest and first commandment. The second is like this: you shall love your neighbor as yourself.' The former is the first, the latter is the second; each is the greatest, since the latter is like the former. Good and sufficient are these twin offspring, since 'upon these depend the whole Law and the Prophets'.* As Paul says: 'the purpose of the precept is charity', which

Ga 5:6

Mt 22:37-40

elsewhere he calls 'the bond of perfection'.*

3. Aptly too the text then refers to a bond of scarlet, the source of the simile in praise of the bride's lips: 'Your lips are like a scarlet ribbon', for her lips are a bond and they glow red when they speak of charity, such fruit of the womb. Charity conceived in the heart, like a flaming fire dyes the lips with a red hue when it bursts through their bonds. Warmth from on high, cast into the heart, lends a kindred color to the lips. What else is meant by saying her lips are as scarlet, except to show that her lips are aflame because scarlet glows with the hue of fire. Her lips no longer need purification with coals from the altar nor cautery with outward fire.* For, already ablaze from an inward flame, her lips plant in others the seed of fire from on high conceived in her womb. Knowledge of salvation indeed they plant, the fiery law which the Lord came to cast upon earth.* Rightly called scarlet are the lips which cast this fire not only upon earth but also up to heaven. In our text, they enkindle even the Lord of heaven. He commends the scarlet lips precisely because they are scarlet for him, because they seem fervent to him, because he perceives them on fire and because they add fire to mutual charity. Here is a surprise: he himself is the fire, yet he catches fire from our sparks. But why not? The Word of God is also a sword,* and none the less he is wounded. 'You have wounded my heart, sister, my bride, you have wounded my heart with one of your eyes.'* Likewise he is also the fire and none the less he is set aflame. He is wounded by an eye, he is set aflame by a lip, and he is even set in bonds; that is why her lips are compared to a ribbon. But charity is the wound, charity is the ribbon, charity is scarlet. Do you see how piercing, how tenacious, how fiery is charity?

In praying use lips like these, bind your Beloved to your heart with the bond of memory as with a tenacious ribbon, fasten him, set him on fire with fervent affection. How sweet if he should say, alluding to you: 'your speech is a passionate fire' and your Bridegroom loves it.* 'Kiss me with the kiss of your mouth',* for your lips are beautiful as a scarlet ribbon, yes, if the desire to kiss is implied in the praise of her lips. He yearns that his lips be imprinted upon yours, that there be one mouth, one pair of lips and that after this imprint he may say to you: This now is mouth of my mouth and lips of my lips. The grace poured upon his lips flows back upon yours and from his scarlet dye your lips also become scarlet. Good is the imprint which communicates such grace to the lips of the bride. Please remember that the lips of which I am speaking now are not lips of the flesh but lips of the spirit, inmost lips of which Paul speaks: 'Sing and make melody in your hearts to the Lord.'* If you are a bride, your lips must be joined and enkindled for this one purpose, to plead with your Beloved, to converse with him, to sing to him, and you may say with the prophet: 'My lips will exult when I sing to you.'* In conversation so holy, let nothing be loose on your lips and then are they like a ribbon; let nothing be chilling, and you have lips of scarlet. Who will grant me, good Jesus, in holding converse with you, to have such lips, so prompt, so open, so enkindled, enkindled and exultant, so as to sing only for you, to sing only of you? Would that my lips were such that through the fine continuity and fervent affection of unbroken meditation they might resemble a bond of scarlet.

Sg 1:1

Eph 5:19

Ps 7:25. Lam 185, n. 96, 188, n. 116.

4. Lips of this kind Christ commends in his bride, not only for prayer but also for exhortation, that she 'may have power to exhort in sound doctrine'.* For lips which bind themselves in colloquy with him, rightly indeed pour out and sow knowledge of salvation; if they resort to sweet and fervent prayer to arouse the hearts of their hearers, scarlet they are, for they cast fire. If however they exhort at the same time as they teach and teach what reflects sound doctrine, what harmonizes with the canons of the faith, at last they are like our ribbon, and the knowledge they disseminate is not only of salvation but also an unbreakable bond.* For what is so self-consistent, so steadfast, woven into such an unbreakable knot as 'the account of our faith'?*

Tt 1:9

Heb 7:16

Rm 12:6

Paul gave such instruction to his disciple when he said: 'Be diligent . . . in exhortation and in teaching'.* But even in ordinary conversation, where mysteries of faith are not formally treated, in just the same way your lips are compared to a scarlet ribbon, if your conversation is delicately measured, discreet, restrained and colored with the pleasing blush of modesty, if both frequently and gladly it alludes to the cross of Christ. O blessed are these lips, truly worthy both of the kiss and the colloquy of Christ! lips so pure and so enkindled, pure in the faith and enkindled in love! This enkindling is from deep within and from the heights, drawing nothing from the abyss.

1 Tm 4:13

5. For there is a kind of enkindling which erupts from the abyss. 'The tongue, a tiny member,' says James, 'sets fire to the whole wheel of our creation, itself catching fire from Gehenna.'* In what good sense can a tongue so badly inflamed kindle a fire? The unstable wheel of corruption from our twisted birth rolls on its own too readily towards evil and plummets headlong by its own impetus; and what need is there to set on fire this wheel which cannot be stopped, but of itself is prone to evil? In fact Scripture notes carefully that 'man's heart is set on evil from his youth'.* Set in motion from its first birth the wheel cannot change its course; and do you with an evil tongue lash and inflame it further? An evil tongue seeks opportunities for wrath and indignation; it either fabricates false insults or exaggerates real insults which it ought to have overlooked; it misconstrues even dutiful performance as an offence and it uses the sparks of poisoned talk to stir up its own heart.* Why with a wicked tongue apply such a wicked tongue apply such a flame to your heart? For the heart let its own flame be enough, the heat of carnal passion and the fever of innate fickleness by which your heart spins like a whirling wheel. Your first birth engendered this flame in you, but the grace of rebirth stunts its growth. Do not add fire to fire and malice to concupiscence. This fire which you vomit, you draw from Gehenna. Thence it begins and

Jm 3:5-6

Gn 8:21

Ws 2:2. Lam 17, n. 69

thither it rushes. 'The tongue is set on fire by Gehenna', says James.* This evil tongue is scarlet, but not a ribbon, for it does not bind but scatters. It enkindles in a bad sense, because it severs what is united, because such a flame rises from the abyss.

Jm 3:6

For[2] the flame 'which comes from above is pure, peaceful, agreeing with the good'* and making others good. 'For a gentle word both multiplies friends and mollifies enemies'.* Like fire it consumes fire. The higher consumes the lower; fire from heaven consumes fire from hell; a wise and pleasant word surpasses a malicious word and a gentle word softens a harsh one. Therefore the Bridegroom says: 'Your lips are like a scarlet ribbon and your speech is enchanting.' For only enchanting words befit the bride, words of love, words which act as a delicate thread, words which will enmesh and draw the Bridegroom with the bonds of charity.[3] Happy the soul which knows how to fasten the mesh of such enchanting words, with which she may ensnare Jesus, bind the Word of the Father with spiritual affections, envelop Christ as it were with wooing words, delay and delight him with loving talk, so that her speech may be pleasant to him who has the words of eternal life and is the eternal Word who lives and reigns with the Father and the Spirit for ever and ever. Amen.

Jm 3:17

Si 6:5

NOTES ON SERMON TWENTY-FOUR

1. G. addresses one person throughout, save for the first word, *audistis*.
2. Reading *Nam* with Migne, mss. Paris 9605, Troyes 419; Mab: *Non*.
3. Ho 11:4, Pr 7:21; this passage seems reminiscent of the Song of Demodocus in the eighth book of the Odyssey.

SERMON 25
PERSONAL PROGRESS

In her modesty the bride does not see her own progress. 1. The countenance reflects the mind and adds charm to the voice. 2. The bride's modesty is praised. 3. Progress is hidden from the individual. 4. The secrets of the bride are hidden within. 5. Some have strange opinions of religious life.

YOUR CHEEKS ARE LIKE BROKEN HALVES OF A POMEGRANATE APART FROM WHAT LIES HIDDEN WITHIN YOU*[1]   *Sg 4:3*

How tasty do you think are the cheeks of the bride, which are edible, since they have the charm of mellow fruit? In fact, you may see even the bodily cheeks of some person full of such pleasing charm that the outer appearance can refresh the minds of the beholders and feed them with the inner charm their appearance suggests.[2] Beauty of countenance speaks for the mind, and the face expresses interior affection.* You see how logically, after white teeth and scarlet lips, the text refers to her cheeks. Cheeks are closely related to lips and when lips are silent the cheeks portray the secrets of the mind by a kind of visible eloquence. Cheeks in turn adopt the function of the voice itself and supplement or add charm to the duty of the voice. However gentle and warm the voice may be, a saucy face makes a charming voice rasp; its levity lessens the seriousness of the message.

2 M 3:16

So the text adds that the demure ripeness of her cheeks enhances the charm of her scarlet lips.

The text tacitly seems to imply some ripeness in her cheeks, since it compares them to a fruit. Ripeness is always appreciated in fruit. In previous verses,* the Canticle described her cheeks as those of a turtle dove,³ because nothing wanton, nothing frivolous, nothing petulant appears in her countenance, but the warmth of her desires may bow down her cheeks with a pleasing seriousness.⁴ Anxious affections do not allow her face to grow wanton and loving meditations banish all levity from her cheeks. Indeed the turtle dove is a fretful bird, a mourning dove. Such Paul wishes the virgin to be, so that she may be anxious 'to please God'* and in the habit of saying: 'My soul has thirsted for God, the living fountain; when shall I come and appear before the face' of the Lord?* Does this not seem to you the voice of one in mourning? Sweet is your mourning, which love has begotten. How are those cheeks not solemn and mellow which affections of mourning have fashioned?

These mournings are more than mournings; they bear also the grace of refreshment. 'You will feed us', says the psalmist, 'with the bread of tears.'* Our text compares the bride's⁵ cheeks to a pomegranate, because her solicitous and loving affection clothes her countenance with a kindred mellowness and feeds those who gaze on her. For the grace of her mind mirrored in her face, as it were, refreshes those who behold her, while she affects them gently and pours into other minds her own passionate love. I cannot fail to be pleasantly moved while in imagination I sketch such a countenance, and her loving cheeks when contemplated beget a similar affection in myself. How much more when they are seen! For sight is more vivid than thought. Utterly beautiful are the cheeks in which such charm is conspicuous, which a welcome humility commends, for they are not puffed up nor do they pout, but by some practice of discipline have been trained to the composure of modest humility.

Sg 1:9

1 Co 7:32

Ps 41:3. Lam 186, nn. 104, 106.

Ps 79:6. Lam 193, n. 153.

2. 'Your cheeks are like broken halves of pomegranate.' Does he not seem to you to have had broken cheeks, who offered them to the strikers and to those who plucked his beard and did not turn from their spittal?* Good indeed is this breaking by which his inner virtue began to be conspicuous and the grace enclosed within the rind of his flesh began to break out. Such surpassing dignity seems to be broken, as it empties itself out for the insults of the passion, but through these broken pieces a cornucopia of salvation was poured out for us. If you also fill up in your flesh what is lacking to Christ's sufferings,* if you bear the stigmata of Christ Jesus in your body,* Christ is already saying to you that 'your cheeks are like broken halves of a pomegranate'. If your cheeks are broken and, as it were, crucified, if they are tamed and trained by a fixed discipline, do they not seem to you like fragments of some goodly fruit? In a later chapter it is said of the Bridegroom: 'his cheeks are like beds of spices',* because they are plowed and harrowed and raked for the cultivation of spices.

Is 50:6

Col 1:24
Ga 6:17

Sg 5:13

So here also the text says that the bride's cheeks are like broken pieces of pomegranate. And good is the breaking by which death does not enter, but an example of spiritual fruit is displayed. Good are the cheeks, then, which have been so broken by humiliation that they do not lose but rather produce the grace of inner fruit. In our text, the pomegranate itself by the red of its rind also denotes the pleasing reserve of a modest countenance. Obviously the finest ornament in the bride of Christ is modesty. Like the dawn, modesty colors the beginnings of all actions and enhances the other virtues with virginal reserve. Modesty does not wantonly boast of its blessings but speaks sparingly, content with a gentle hint when need demands. Good Jesus, what modesty there is everywhere in your speech! How sparing you are in your own praises, which you could have appositely articulated as much without loss of humility as without harm to the truth! And when he expressed his own blessings, still he suppressed his own name. He could have spoken more fully, but to set the bride an example, he himself assumed the color of modest reserve.

I am not now promoting the modesty which tinges the face with a visible blush, but that which enhances the features of one's whole way of life. For as one's face has cheeks, so one's whole way of life has similar features, in which nothing is more pleasing than the color, if the character of every act is redolent of humility, if it hides more in the heart than it shows on the face. In our text also the Bridegroom says: 'Your cheeks are like broken pieces of pomegranate, apart from what lies hidden within you.' Good are the cheeks which, as they present no false front, so possess much hidden treasure, as they offer nothing counterfeit, so do not squander their reserve; they display less in appearance than their inner reserve of virtue.

3. These qualities can be applied to the inner cheeks of the soul which are upon the face of conscience, where not man but God beholds. Each one's conscience has as it were, a face of its own.[6] One's cheeks blush with the modest hue of humility, if in one's heart one would not boast of good works, would not exaggerate merits, would not consider them outstanding but would be ashamed that they are so trivial. For who will pride himself on having a chaste heart?* If he has received this gift, how will he boast as if he had not received it?* Yet who understands the very gifts he has received? For if he does not understand his faults,* how much less his gifts? Gifts are from above, they come down from the Father of lights.* But 'no one except the Spirit of God comprehends the thoughts of God'.† Therefore if God reveals himself to anyone through his Spirit, it is not so much the man himself who knows, as the Spirit of God within him. 'We have received . . . the Spirit which is from God', says Paul, 'that we might understand the gifts bestowed on us by God.'* Does this mean all gifts? Or if one could understand all gifts, could one understand all gifts in every respect? Not even one gift, I think, in its entirety; and if the

Pr 20:9
1 Co 4:7

Ps 18:13

Jm 1:17;
see G. T 5.

†1 Co 2:11

1 Co 2:12

gift were hidden in a scourge, one could not understand that gift at all.*   *Jb 19:6*

Conscience itself is profitably hidden from itself in part, and an excessive love of making progress is itself ignorant of the advances of its own progress. In our text not the fulness of virtues as of whole pomegranates but only slices are said to appear in the bride's cheeks, for what is on the cheeks is apparent. And if one recognizes the grace of some virtue really present within oneself, is one aware of its intensity, its steadfastness, its perseverance? 'My frame was not hidden from you', says the psalmist, 'when I was being made in secret.'* Though it be hidden from me,   *Ps 138:15* it is not hidden from you, for your 'Spirit searches everything' even what is hidden in me.* Would that I   *1 Co 2:10* might have many such gifts hidden in me, known to you, good Jesus, and stored among your treasures. Perilous it is to store them in my understanding; therefore I entrust them more safely to yours. Yet it it not so much I who entrust them to you as you who do not entrust them to me. In your keeping you cherish still more safely what you have made in secret. Nor is so much perfection in the bride allowed to be disclosed to her and to appear on her cheeks in its fulness.

4. 'Thus are your cheeks, apart from what lies hidden within you.'* Some secrets are to be brought   *Sg 6:6* to light at a suitable time and displayed on the face. Meanwhile they lie hidden germinally, destined to receive their full beauty in due time. Now therefore you are a bride, but it is not yet apparent what you will be.* In your opinion, who will be like Me when I   *1 Jo 3:2* appear? Even now you have a partial likeness, because you know partially.* 'With face unveiled' you   *1 Co 13:9* are 'already contemplating my glory', but yet you are still 'being transformed from one degree of glory to another'.* While you are being transformed, you do   *2 Co 3:18* not yet possess wholly. To be transformed is to make progress, but not yet to have been made perfect. Your perfection, however, is not yet yours, but already my eyes see it; with me you already are such as you will be, O bride. Already you have been written in the

book of life and I have your portrait in my hands. Your face is before me always; it shines bright before me, though in you at present it is obscured. Already I have found the drachma of my image in you, but it is still coated with rust and its beauty is hidden. Faith already glows on your cheeks and suffuses them with the color of life, but the object of faith is in hiding. That is why 'your cheeks are like broken halves of a pomegranate, apart from what lies hidden within you'. Pleasing enough is the countenance of your faith, but you appear to me more praiseworthy for what is hidden within you. The virtue of patience, plain to see and as if on your cheeks, is already pleasing enough, but I value you more for the glory to come.

And truthfully, brothers, the sufferings—no, I do not say sufferings, but even the endurance—of this present time is 'not worth comparing with the glory that is to be revealed in us'.* Of that glory some seeds have already been sown in us, which by a hidden working are bringing themselves to maturity and to the substance of a perfect fruit. This substance is at present hidden in us by a kind of grace proper to seeds. 'My substance', says the psalmist, 'is in the lower parts of the earth.'* Do you see where he says his substance is hidden? 'In the lower parts of the earth.' Luckily for him, his substance is not in the lowest parts. Personally I understand that there are some upper, some lower, and some lowest parts of the earth. The upper parts are the very nature of the human body; the lower parts are what is corrupt in the same nature; the lowest parts are some iniquity and fault proceeding from corruption and corrupting nature still more. The prophet does not say that his substance is in the lowest parts, precisely because that spiritual grace (which for the prophet is the highest substance) has no truck with iniquity; he says rather 'in the lower parts of the earth'. 'My substance', because for its healing effect the grace of the Spirit is hidden in the weakness of the flesh, and concealed like leaven grace continues its work of healing until mortality is swallowed up by life.* For the lump of

Rm 8:18

Ps 138:15

2 Co 5:4

dough should not corrupt the leaven but rather be changed by the leaven into a similar flavor.* Ga 5:9

5. Elsewhere too the psalmist also says: 'My substance is with you.'* Therefore his substance is both in the lower parts of the earth and with the Lord. It is hidden in far distance places, in the heights of heaven and in the lower parts of earth, in eternity and in infirmity, there by Providence, here by grace active within. Good is the grace which so effects progress in virtue that in turn it breathes into us a taste for perfection and divulges secrets hidden from the beginning of the world,* hidden to the world and hidden in God, where our 'life has been hidden with Christ'.* And truly 'great is the wealth of your sweetness, O Lord, which you have hidden from those who fear you',* but not from those who love you. So perhaps this sweetness does not escape the attention of the bride.* These very secrets belong to the bride, for of them the Bridegroom says: 'Such are your cheeks, apart from what lies hidden within you.' Ps 38:8
Mt 13:35
Col 3:3
Ps 30:20
Tb 2:21

This statement was made then not for her alone, but for the bystanders, or even more for those standing far off and for those who stand opposed, for those who through fear retreat from a holy way of life and for those who through envy defame it.* Some among them consider the hidden life, the life of the saints, empty and without honor. Some others without considering it empty, still regard its whole direction with utmost horror, for they dare not entertain the suspicion that its ending is without honor.* The former consider religious life empty, the latter consider it bitter. The former do not respect it, the latter fear to draw near. Therefore the Bridegroom took pains to hint delicately at the secrets of the bride, as if indirectly touching the envious and attracting the timorous, while giving some veiled intimation of her inmost delights as follows: 'Such are your cheeks, apart from what lies hidden within you'; as if he were to say: if others also knew with what hidden treasures your interior is filled, O bride, how readily they would reckon all else as loss in order to gain those treasures!* How gladly they Lam 13, n. 47.

Ws 5:4, Lam 14, n. 52.

Ph 3:7-8 would both forfeit the good and endure the evil to becomes sharers in that hidden sweetness!

Now, however, hidden from their eyes is the sweetness which intermittently bursts in upon holy souls in secret. Agreeable indeed is this ebb and flow which mitigates the hardships of many seasons, and not negligible are these delights which flow into seasons to come. Why do you fear want in seasons to come? There are delights in the bride's secrets and abounding delights. Now there is abundance in your towers, O bride, for the text says: 'your neck is like the tower of David',* and if her delights lie hidden, her virtue is conspicuous. How is it not conspicuous, when it is compared to a tower? But let us postpone this for tomorrow's sermon, when we shall say about this tower what the real David gives us, its author and our tutor, Jesus Christ, who lives and reigns for ever and ever. Amen.

NOTES ON SERMON TWENTY-FIVE

1. G. is writing for one individual, though once, par. 4, he interjects *fratres*. See also Sg 6:6.
2. Read *internos* with Mab., Paris 9605, Troyes 419; Migne: *inter nos*.
3. See Is 59:11; Bernard, SC 59:3-6; Morson, 162-3; White, 144-46.
4. *desideriorum aestus dulci gravitate deiiciat,* Mab; *dejiciat,* Migne.
5. Reading *sponsae* with mss. Paris 9605, Troyes 419; Mab. and Migne: *sponsi*.
6. Reading with Mab: *quamdam;* mss Paris 9605, Troyes 419: *quandam;* Migne: *quadam.*

SERMON 26
BATTLEMENTS OF THE WORD
AND OF CHARITY

The bride is protected by battlements of the word and of charity. 1. The bride is beautiful and brave, free from the yoke of Adam for the yoke of Christ. 2. To the yoke of Adam we add yokes of oxen; the flame of concupiscence we stoke with flames from its smithy. 3. The yoke of Christ with its chrism breaks the yoke of oxen and rots the knots of enslavement. 4. The bride borrows from her Bridegroom to build her tower of humility. 5. Against siege without and famine within, charity is her rampart. 6. From charity spring solicitude, prudence and wariness; the shields of charity are an orderly life, the rule, and the word of God, 7. but especially the shield of the word of God. 8. Charity has four shields: the shield of faith, the shield of truth, the shield of good will, the shield of the sacred word. 9. The bride towers upwards in the ecstasy of contemplation and bends to suckle her young.

YOUR NECK IS LIKE THE TOWER OF DAVID, BUILT WITH BATTLEMENTS. A THOUSAND SHIELDS HANG FROM IT, ALL THE ARMOR OF VALIANT MEN*[1] *Sg* 4:4

The Bridegroom at last discourses on brave deeds to the bride and about the bride; previously he spoke of her charms, for instance: 'Your neck is like a jewelled necklace'.* You have something similar in a psalm: 'The Lord has robed himself in beauty, he has robed himself in strength.'* Good are these robes, one an elegant mantle, the other a coat of mail. He placed first the robe which seems more appropriate to the bride. Now he addresses himself, as it were, to her fortitude. The virtue of fortitude in the bride is as much more precious as it is more rare. Rare it is obviously, for who shall find a valiant woman?* And if one can be found, still you, good Jesus, do not so much find her valiant, as you come beforehand to make her so. This very tower does not build itself, but he builds it, without whom the builders labor in vain.*

See how valiant he wishes her to be considered, when he compares her to the tower of David. 'Your neck', he says, 'is like the tower of David.' Do not attribute inflexibility and hardness to this neck, for these qualities cannot be matter for praise but rather call down a curse. 'Cursed be their rage,' says the Scripture, 'because it is stubborn, and their wrath because it is hard.'* 'Your neck', says Isaiah, 'is an iron sinew.'* These statements are directed towards condemnation, not elicited for commendation! Unbending obstinacy is wont to counterfeit the liberty which I understand in these words: 'Your neck is like the tower of David.'

Her neck is obviously free, unacquainted with the state of slavery, as erect and as fortified as David's tower. I do not think this neck will be chafed by any yoke of abject servility. 'Heavy is the yoke upon the children of Adam' from the day of their birth,* but the bride no longer seems one of the daughters of Adam. She has already exchanged her ancient birth for the newness of regeneration, and now is unacquainted with the carnal Adam, for from him she passed over to Christ; from him she has cleaved to the second Adam and become one spirit with Him.* For this reason she is free, because 'where the spirit of the Lord is, there is freedom' and 'the freedom with which Christ set us free', a freedom freely given, not inborn.* For from their birth 'heavy is the yoke upon the children of Adam'. It is really heavy, for this yoke kept that woman in the Gospel bent double for eighteen years, not allowing her to look up,* utterly unlike the bride here, who has raised her neck like a tower towards heaven.   *Lk 13:11*

2. Heavy clearly was the yoke which the whole human race, personified in this woman but bent double, could not shake off. Mankind could not lay aside the yoke and it did not cease to lay wrong upon wrong and weakness upon weakness, and each upon the other, in a fertile but most unfortunate harvesting. Would you hear of mankind laying yoke upon yoke? Hear on what pretext an invited guest in the Gospel excused himself from the supper: 'I have bought five yoke of oxen'.* O senseless soul,   *Lk 14:14*
with so feeble a neck and a nape so chafed! One yoke you bear which your corrupt birth imposed on you, and are you buying more? You need not purchase what is freely yours by birth. You are bidding to buy others, while you cannot free your neck from this which oppresses you. 'I have bought five yoke of oxen', you say, and without ransom you cannot shake off this yoke so heavy and so universal. Nor can you yet afford the price of your redemption. Do you not know with what a heavy yoke you are harnessed? It cannot be lifted except by the blood of Christ. You have plenty for buying more yokes but not enough to redeem yourself from this. O wretched riches of yours! You are rich enough not to relieve but to multiply the halters for your neck and to make your fetters more galling.

Let that heavy yoke by which you are oppressed be enough for you. This yoke, if you do not know, is some compulsion to do wrong and an impossibility of rising again. This yoke is an unreadiness for good and a passion for evil. This yoke is both the wrongdoing for which you are held liable to punishment and the weakness by which you are dragged headlong into vice. These are yours from your origin and transmitted through procreation, and you increase your load with burdens freely accepted! While through the curiosity of your five senses[2] you hasten towards outward show, you stir up an inward flame of concupiscence which can only be extinguished by the blood of Christ. Concupiscence undisturbed burns well enough, but stoked with fuel from without concupiscence rages out of control. Here is a double provocation: the corruption of nature and a kind of curiosity probing to awaken it from without. Here is a doubled nuisance: one's own impulse and an enemy's assault; a doubled nuisance: the flame of concupiscence and the bellows of its smithy.

3. 'I have bought five yoke of oxen.' 'Of oxen' is aptly said, for the toil of curiosity galls dull minds. If you want a yoke you have no need to bid for one. Take upon yourself the yoke of Christ, a yoke not for purchase, a pleasant yoke, not a ponderous yoke. 'For my yoke is gentle', says the Lord, 'and my burden light.'* This yoke is not a yoke of oxen, since it is a yoke of reason,* a yoke which does not impose toil but procures rest. Observe also how he says this yoke is light. For that previous one is heavy, which is 'upon the children of Adam'* from the day of their birth to the day of their death. Of what death, do you think? To be sure, that of which Paul says: 'You have died and your life is hidden with Christ in God.'* Good is this death which buries the old birth and brings in a new birth. Good is this death which swallows slavery and begets freedom. For the children of this birth are free. Good is this ending, that while discarding the old Adam, we may simultaneously cast off his heavy yoke. This ending of the life of the flesh breaks the yoke of our captivity; it can gall us no longer but it rots from the effects of the oil from the time we begin to be called by another name and over us is invoked the name of the second Adam, for his name is like oil poured out.*

Would you hear of both the breaking and the rotting of this heavy yoke? 'He forgives all your sins, he heals all your infirmities.'* Sin is pardoned wholly, once for all; the yoke has been broken. Infirmity is still being healed; the yoke is rotting. In the text, what is rotting wastes away slowly, does not disappear all at once. The resolve of the will can indeed be cut through and, as it were, broken, but deep-rooted passion is not so much cut out as unlearned. And when the impossibility of working out our salvation is removed by grace, then, as it were, the yoke of captivity is broken. But the difficulty in achieving goodness still lingers; while the difficulty is gradually being healed, its yoke is decaying. 'It will rot', says Isaiah,* and he allows the implication that, if not all at once, yet eventually it is to be consumed by decay. What decays is surely destroyed! How is he not free, whose yoke is either broken at once or gradually destroyed? Both a yoke and a rope, each when broken seems robbed of its purpose, for neither can a broken yoke grievously oppress nor a rotten rope firmly bind. Happy surely is the one whose bonds have so rotted that they are useless, whose chains have decayed and rotted from the action of the oil. *Is 10:27*

4. But you will say: you had begun to talk about the neck of the bride, why do you linger over a yoke? What connection is there between the yoke and the neck? I wish there were none! But in fact the galling is intense. What is a yoke meant for, save the neck? Yet not for the neck of the bride, since the bonds have already been loosed from her neck and she knows no constraint from the yoke of slavery. 'Your neck is like the tower of David', says the Bridegroom. By this is indicated the most towering liberty, liberty free of all oppression, yet not sheer liberty with no fibre of strength. In a tower one expects not only height but also the strength of ramparts against the face of the foe. Freedom has indeed been restored but security is not yet allowed you. The snare of captivity has been broken.* The enemy seeks to trap you from another quarter; he has lost his claim, but he has not abandoned the hope of regaining it, nor his determination to attack. You have been set free, but henceforth the responsibility of guarding your freedom falls on you. Do not, even in the slightest way, let your neck, surrendered to the embraces of the Bridegroom, be exposed to any degenerate yoke. *Ps 123:7*

According to Luke, the father meeting his son at his return fell upon his neck. Dear was the burden and gentle the yoke though the son did not deserve to bear or to feel it until, first restored to his right mind, he broke with his state of slavery and so returned to his father.* Your neck is upright; be strong as the tower of David, that you may say: 'I will guard my strength for you.'* For he is David, he is Solomon, Christ, that is, the power of God and the wisdom of God.* You are his tower if you have no lowly and feeble idea of him, provided your towering ideas come from the power of God and not from yourself. He is like a tower, not the tower of David but a tower opposed to David who, 'puffed up with the opinions of his own flesh', exalts 'himself in opposition to the knowledge of God'.* Lofty is this neck but wisdom tramples on the necks of the proud and lofty and exalts those of the humble.*

Humility itself supplies the funds needed to build the tower of the Gospel. Nor should one be embarrassed lest funds fail the bride, for they can be borrowed liberally from the treasury of the Bridegroom: 'Learn of me', he says, 'for I am meek and humble of heart.'* Do you not yet understand how humility supplies funds for the building of the tower? 'The man who humbles himself', says the Lord, 'shall be exalted.'* Aptly there was a hidden suggestion about humility in a previous verse, where the Bridegroom mentions what was hidden in the bride, since it is a beautiful example of humility to conceal the praises of one's merits.* If there he speaks of her humility, here as a consequence he adds a note about her loftiness. A tower founded upon humility cannot be hidden long.

5. 'Your neck is like the tower of David.' Consider the privilege of the bride. The apostle Peter exhorts us to be built together 'into a spiritual home',* but the bride is built not only into a home but also into a tower. Paul wishes us to be built together 'into a dwelling-place of God',* but the bride, not satisfied with this, adds battlements also, that her dwelling-place may be lofty and more

secure. Perhaps hers is also one of those towers of which it is said: 'Let peace be in your power and plenty in your towers.'* It is altogether fitting that plenty be not lacking in a tower. Harsh is the need because it is doubled when there is a siege without and famine within. What does it profit that the entrances are all closed and barred, if famine, that savage within, spreads universal grief? *Ps 121:7*

Disaffection is an evil famine. The gates have been closed and the outer approaches barred, if death makes no entry through the windows of the senses and if the probing of the rebellious senses does not welcome provocation to evil from foreign imports. If you 'spurn profit from extortion', if you 'stop your ears from suggestions of murder', if you 'shut your eyes to the sight of evil',* you are already enclosed, already you dwell on the heights and your elevation is a bastion of rocks. But is that enough? Of what use is such a well-fortified height, if famine and the cruel hunger of disaffection ravages what is within? Of what uses is the solid and steep height of rock, if no bread is there, if wells can run dry? *Is 31:15*

Good indeed is a stronghold, if rations hold out. Good is a fortress of granite, if it be such that from its hard substance honey and oil may be extracted. And indeed the very hardness of observances and the rock of discipline often pour full streams of oil, and the somewhat stony rigor of our Order supplies sweetness of devotion to the jowls of the mind.³ In the words of the Psalm: 'Let peace be in your power and plenty in your towers', Jerusalem, but 'a plenty for those who love you.'* Otherwise, one who does not love, though he be within, goes hungry none the less. *Ps 121:7*

But how shall there be want in this spiritual tower, in the tower of David, in the neck of the bride, through which in unending exchange the spirit of life is drawn in and breathed out, the supply line of the divine word is unbroken, and the breath of the voice ever flows? How shall there be famine in the neck through which an abundance of sweetness and the word of goodness surges from the free fountain of the heart? The neck seems to resemble both a channel and a bond both between the heart and the lips, and between the body and the head, and between all four. In the neck is both a bond and a way. What else is the bond to be, save charity, by which the body is joined to the head, the Church to Christ? What else is the way of the spirit to be, save charity? For this is 'the more excellent way', or rather this is the spirit which comes and goes and returns to its source, going back to the place of its birth.* On this depend the Law and the Prophets†

6. Therefore 'a thousand shields hang from it'. For every word of the Lord is a flaming shield and the battlements themselves are related to speech. In a later chapter we read: 'If she is a wall, let us build upon it battlements of silver.'* Battlements are usually of the same material as the tower and form one body with it. And consider how charity supports battlements of the same substance and body as itself. Consider how there is inborn in charity a kind of solicitude, prudence and watchful wariness to avoid or repel assaults and stratagems of the foe. Battlements have open crenels and closed merlons. Through the crenels, charity detects ambushes; through the merlons it diverts assaults; through the one charity forsees, through the other it protects. Charity has been built with such battlements because such solicitude, so strong and so prudent, is inborn in it. Charity is a great support for itself. In fact love is strong as a tower. It knows the opportunities for assault, knows when there is need for retreat, but when there is no possibility of retreat, it knows how to endure with courage. Although it seems to have so much support in itself, it does not refuse assistance from others. Fortified with battlements, charity also takes up shields. A good shield is an orderly way of life and a law transmitted by men. Although this is not necessary to charity, it is not considered superfluous or even burdensome. Charity is of the spirit; it needs no law, yet it does not disdain law but uses it as law should be used, being protected and not oppressed by

law. A good shield also is meditation on the sacred word, for 'every word' of the Lord 'is a flaming shield'.* *Pr 30:5. Lam 182, n. 71; n. 170.*

7. Charity is not content with the spiritual meditations which it begets itself and although it is itself the law of the Lord, it meditates on the very words of the Law;⁴ thence it derives its credentials, thence it guards and protects itself on Sion with a manifold shield.⁵ Although charity has within itself the great witness of the Spirit,* still it seeks protection for itself from the sacred writings. Good is the protection which either the experience of charity suggests or skill in the divine word transmits. In his Epistle, Paul depicts for you some battlements of charity: 'Charity is patient', he says, 'it is kind.' Read through the entire passage about charity; does it not seem to you that as many battlements rise up as the distinct graces he lists? 'Charity is not jealous, does not act perversely, is not boastful, is not ambitious; charity does not insist on its own way, does not take pleasure in wrongdoing but rejoices in the right', and so forth as far as, 'charity never ends'.* *1 Jo 5:7-8. Miquel 152, n. 6. Lam 182, n. 72.*

1 Co 13:4-8

Do you see with what a crown of battlements charity is built? Do these battlements not seem to form one body with charity and rise as it were from its foundation? And yet these affections to which charity, as it were, gives birth by its nature, education directs, discipline governs, and practice exalts; and this good originating with charity, this way of life drawn up by experts, either encourages lest it grow weak or inspires that it may grow strong. So charity, not content with inward inspiration, hangs in the memory the directives of sacred Scripture like shields displayed on all sides. Behold the Bridegroom himself, who is the mediator and negotiator between men and God, as the neck communicates between the body and the head, 'a tower of strength against the enemy',* behold him I say, who though rich in shields of his own assumed the shields of Scripture and, as it were, had recourse to its authority to check with the shield of truth the wily assaults of a malicious interpreter. *Ps 60:4. Lam 182, n. 73.*

8. If you also are a mediator and a negotiator between men and God, and like a neck join body and head, let a thousand shields be buckled around you, the manifold shields of the divine word. Let sacred authority be ready at hand and for every engagement let it be your patron, not only to satisfy yourself but also to enrich others. Be ready to render to everyone who asks an account of the faith and hope that are in you.* He seems to demand an account of your faith, who tries to promote what is contrary to the faith and to trespass upon it. A good shield therefore hangs from your neck, if you are protected with the shield of truth, the shield of good will, the shield of the sacred word. You read of all these shields in the Scriptures. But if you are also like a tower raised on high by charity, if by the grace of contemplation, like a neck rising about the rest of the body, you approach the Lord's head and are hidden in the secret of his face, in the enclave of the Bridegroom, in the bridal chamber of truth, do you not seem to be protected by an ornate shield?

I know not whether any shield is a greater guarantee of protection than such an embrace of the Beloved. This is a fiery* shield and therefore it extinguishes all the fiery shafts of the foe of foes, and its fire devours fire. If the shield of faith extinguishes those shafts, how much more is he protected by the trusty shield of truth, who is hidden in the warmth of its embrace? For meditation upon truth is fervent,[6] and it extinguishes the evilly enkindled suggestions of the enemy before they can reach the mind. Between her embraces of the Bridegroom and her duties of charity, there is no time for the bride to be struck by stray shafts.[7] Such a shield is a neat pendant from the neck of the bride because love alone experiences the grace of so warm an embrace, love alone knows such transports and, making the mind cleave to God, for a space fuses it into one spirit with him.* Blessed surely is the neck wherein dwells the fiery word of the Lord, from which hangs like a shield in delightful embrace the Word of the Father, his truth and his power. Does he not seem to

1 P 3:15; to Peter's words, G. adds: [fide et] spe, as in S 16:4. Lam 1 79.

Na 2:3

1 Co 6:17

you delightfully protected, who on all sides before and behind is crowned and surrounded by such shields?

For believers there is a trusty peg, from which hang weapons of so many different kinds. Neatly they hang from the neck of charity, since it is the unction which teaches us and suggests all things,* since upon it all graces are conferred, to it all are referred and by its measure all are considered and weighed. 'A thousand shields hang from it, all the armor of valiant men.' Surely this is the armor of Paul's inventory to the Ephesians.* 'All the armor of valiant men', that is of lovers for 'love is strong as death.'* What follows? Is only the armor of the valiant there, and no breasts for infants? If charity soars like a tower, does charity not bend down? 'If we are out of our senses, it is for God; if we are in our right mind, it is for you. The charity of Christ impels us.'*

Jo 14:26

Ep 6:13-18

Sg 8:6

2 Co 5:13-14

9. You have heard of the bride out of her senses; would you hear of her also when she is in her right senses and bends down? 'Your two breasts are like two fawns, twins of a gazelle.'* A good tower is the bride; on all sides she encloses herself with the discipline of an ordered life; and she has pendant from her neck a wealth of shields in the teachings of Scripture, and she rises to the heights in her transports of contemplation. Likewise her self-restraint is strong, her teaching reliable and her ecstasy heavenly; yet her loftiness has also learned to bend down to our level, the richness of her teaching to be brought down to sobriety, her austerity to melt, as it were, into the sweetness of spiritual milk,* and the armor of the valiant to be transformed into breasts for the weak. Everywhere the charity of Christ prompts her, sweeping her upwards to himself and drawing her downwards for his sake, but not detaining her overlong before, to her delight, she hastens directly towards ecstasy.

Sg 4:5-6. See Morson, 161-2, White 42-3.

1 P 2:2

So the Bridegroom says: 'Your breasts are like two fawns, twins of a gazelle',* because she ever gazes towards the mountains of her pastureland,

Sg 4:5

because her wonted refreshment lures and carries her to the realm of her pastureland, because with graceful leap she suddenly bounds towards the lilies of the Bridegroom, whence delightfully nourished on the juices of heavenly herbs, she repeatedly brings back breasts filled for her young. But what must be said about these breasts, ears perhaps weary and the fleeting hour cannot now endure. There is now no time for a drink of milk pressed from those breasts. When the Lord, thanks to your prayers, offers more plentiful leisure and more ample time, I shall not refuse you the ministry of my lips, if he who grants his affection will also grant the eloquence to praise him, Christ Jesus, who with the Father and the Holy Spirit lives and reigns for ever and ever. Amen.

NOTES TO SERMON TWENTY-SIX

1. Written for one person throughout.
2. On curiosity of the senses, see Lam 184, n. 92.
3. On *disciplina* here and in S 26:9, see Lam 170, nn. 3, 5.
4. Mab., mss. Paris 9605, Troyes 419: *meditatur;* Migne: *mediatur.* Lam 185, n. 99.
5. Ps 19:3, 2, gives a basis for restoring the text to read: *inde se de Sion tuetur et multiplici protegit clypeo.* Mab. and Migne read *inde se (al. sensa) tuetur;* Dion reads: *inde* tuetur;* Vulg. reads: *et de Sion tuetur te,* with *protegat te,* in the preceding verse; mss. Paris 9605: *sensa tuetur;* Troyes 419: *? sensa tuetur.*
6. On *meditatio veritatis* see Lam 183, n. 78; on *fervida meditatio,* Lam 185, n. 102.
7. Possibly a reminiscence of Vergil, *Aeneid,* 4:69-72.

SERMON 27

RAPTUROUS FEAST

AND THE MILK OF BABES

The bride feasts on spiritual food to give milk to her babes. 1. The Church, through Paul, gave the milk of babes to both Jew and Gentile, for her compassion cares and her adaptation cures. 2. Paul's example should be followed for true eloquence. 3. The Church treats the fawns as twins in grace, both Jew and Gentile. 4. Her lilies are models of chastity and of the sacred word. 5. The bride who feeds on the heights feeds her twins from comely breasts. 6. The vision and pleasures of pre-dawn give place to eternal day. 7. In the repose of night, the fawns are refreshed because they graze on delightful lilies until daybreak.

YOUR TWO BREASTS ARE LIKE TWO FAWNS, TWINS OF A GAZELLE, WHICH GRAZE AMID THE LILIES, UNTIL THE DAY BREAKS AND THE SHADOWS VANISH.[1]* *Sg 4:5-6*

You see, brothers, how not even the breasts of the bride are bereft of praise. Indeed mention of breasts is frequent both elsewhere and especially in these Songs. The Bridegroom prefers breasts to wine,* compares them to a cluster of grapes,* likens them to a tower,* and says in the passage now before us: 'Your two breasts are like two fawns, twins of a gazelle which graze amid the lilies.' You see in how many ways her breasts are praised. If the bride is a mother, her breasts are a comely need for her maternal bosom. Paul knew the need for breasts, when he said: 'We become babes among you, like a nurse

Sg 1:1
Sg 7:7
Sg 8:10

taking care of her children.'* Does he not seem to you to have become like a fawn, who has become like a babe? How did he foster his children like a nurse, if he did not have breasts?

Like two fawns of a gazelle are the two sons of the Church: one from circumcision, the other from the Gentiles. Notice how Paul adapts his breasts to both. 'To the Jews I became as a Jew . . . ; to those outside the Law . . . I have become all things to all, in order to gain all.'* Did he not adapt his breasts to these fawns when he became all things to all men? He became all things to all men, not with the cunning of a hypocrite but with the affection of one who has compassion and with the bearing of one who adapts himself. In our context, he conformed himself to both, now with the Jews abstaining from what was lawful, now with the Gentiles partaking of what was lawful, everywhere avoiding offence to either race where no harm to the faith deterred him. He became all things to all men, neither robbing the Jews of rites still lawful at the beginning, nor forcing the Gentiles into a mockery of the Jews. He became all things to all men, according to the capacity of his hearers both giving moral precepts and explaining mysteries. In these two subjects he proferred as it were two breasts, providing his babes with the milk of simpler teaching.

Inner compassion does indeed possess breasts, but adaptation exhibits them outwardly. Compassion cares, but adaptation cures. For what does it profit me, if you show only compassion and are unable to adapt yourself to suit my weakness and, so to speak, to my infancy? What does it profit me, if by your feelings of compassion you make my cause your own, but do not provide the care you ought? Both are necessary, not only compassion but also some adaptation of discipline and teaching. Compassion brings your feelings into conformity, adaptation makes you stoop to feed your babes with milk for their needs. In neither way do holy teachers fail their hearers; they become like their hearers both in the affection of piety and in the practice of adaptation.

1 Th 2:7

1 Co 9:20-22; ut omnes lucrifaciam; *Vulg:* ut omnes facerem salvos.

2. Would that those who are to preach in the assembly of the brethren would attend to this. They are bent on grandiloquence rather than on relevance. They make prodigies of themselves among people of weak understanding without effecting their salvation. They blush to teach humble and simple truths, lest they should seem to know only these. They blush to have breasts, to bare the breast, to give milk to their babes. What does this mean? Did you take your place in their midst, filling a pulpit that you might display your learning or that you might give milk to your subjects in their tender infancy? You weave subtleties; the listeners marvel at your art; they praise your eloquence. That is fair enough, provided they are touched by grace, provided as you argue, the affections of your listeners are moved and their understanding instructed. Otherwise, why introduce subjects foreign to the business in hand, which your hearers may not understand?

A great tribute to eloquence is to prosecute expertly the case you have undertaken, to refer everything to its advantage, to support the business in hand. Nowhere will you give a more obvious sign of your eloquence than if you develop ordinary material artistically. By the charm of your talk you may resurrect what by itself seemed dead and, as it were, turn thoughts that went begging into nobler ideas. Pay less attention to what suits your style as a man of letters and more to what they should hear whom you are instructing. For why should they follow after you, if you promenade over highways and wonderways, I do not say above you but above those in the pew?* Do not broach a lofty subject in a lofty style, but bend down to the humble.* *Ps 130:1* *Rm 11:20; 12:16*

When you talk of sublime subjects out of due season, what else do you seem to desire but that men be struck dumb before you alone and that what was said of the Saviour be said of you: 'Never has a man so spoken'?* You have climbed into the pulpit to edify others, not to inflate yourself; to fill others, not to empty yourself, except perhaps in the way of the Saviour 'emptied himself, taking the form of a *Jn 7:46* servant',* in order to nourish us for our salvation with the milk of his flesh. A good imitator of his Master, Paul does not conceal his breasts but boasts of having them: 'As babes in Christ I gave you not solid food but milk to drink', and likewise: 'I decided to know nothing among you except Jesus Christ and him crucified.'* He knows for whom he is setting the table and to whom he is proffering his breasts. So his breasts are like those of a fawn because the breasts[2] of his teaching are softened, such as babes in Christ can grasp.

3. Now you have heard what these fawns are and why there are two. Would you know why they are twins? Because in the faith there is no distinction between a Jew and a Greek.* Your privileges of merit are abolished and rebirth confers distinction on no one, for rebirth absolves all alike. For all 'fall short of the glory of God and are justified by his grace as a gift'.* Faith ennobles both peoples alike but the Jew thinks otherwise and in the kindness shown to all he claims rights peculiar to himself. What wonder if he seeks to be the first, when he sought to be the only one? He cannot be the only-begotten; so he strives to be at least the first-born. See how many objections were brought against Peter in the Acts of the Apostles, because he had visited uncircumcised men and admitted them into the mysteries of the faith.* See how Paul in the Epistle of the Romans toils in the sweat of his brow against the Jews, because in grace they claimed certain privileges of the faith for themselves and tried to divide into classes those whom one faith joined together.* They pretended in Acts to be the only ones in grace, but in Romans the highest in grace; they were unwilling to admit to equality those whom they could not fail to have as partners. But God made the Gentiles of one body with Israel and sharers of both covenants, making no distinction in any one, cleansing their hearts by faith.*

So they are called twins, because faith does not separate into classes those whom faith regenerates without exception. Contrariwise, those who know not how to be twins have been made nobodies, and though once they occupied the first place at the banquet, they no longer have even the last. This plan not only applies to them but extends to all, so that no one, whatever his rank, should envy another's partnership or equality in grace. For who should allege merits, where grace is entirely in giving? Events of old must not sway the scale, where everything has been made new. As newness of rebirth is suggested in the fawns, so equality of rebirth is suggested in the twins. Appropriately they are said to belong to a gazelle, that is, to be children of the Church, especially because—like gazelles—they have keen vision. Keen are the eyes of the Church, because she contemplates 'not what is seen but what is unseen'.* *2 Co 4:18*

4. 'Your two breasts are like two fawns, twins of a gazelle, which graze amid the lilies', provided of course they experience the grace of lilies, provided for them lilies have the fragrance of lilies and do not emit a rank odor. Good and pleasing is the fragrance of a lily, yet the same lily for some has the perfume of a lily, for others the malodor of wormwood. The lily of the valley, the lily unique is Christ; lilies were persons who imitated him. Hear what one of those lilies says: 'We are the fair aroma of Christ, . . . to some a fragrance from death to death, to others a fragrance from life to life.'* You see how unique is *2 Co 2:15-16* that lily in which the fulness of all things good breathed perfume, but to some seemed malodorous. The latter turn bitter to sweet and darkness to light.

But he truly grazes amid lilies, who masters the fragrance of lilies. Lilies are the models of chastity which, not only in our day and in our presence but also in times past and in distant places, breathe out the fairest fragrance. Lilies are also holy words, in which we scent the joys of eternal life and draw in the breath of perfumes. With how many such lilies, brothers, have you been surrounded! Though all the children of the Church have been blessed, you have been blessed more luxuriantly. For into your nostrils at almost every moment the chaste utterances, now of prophets, now of apostles, now of evangelists, breathe forth like lilies, and their words and life are perfumed with an enchanting aroma. For what lilies could waft a sweeter scent, what lilies could rival their fragrance? What perfume does Mary breathe upon you, and John and Peter and the other men in the Gospel, and what finally does Jesus himself, who as no other both radiates fragrance in his own person and alone is personally perceived in all others, however sweet-scented be their perfume!

His words waft a new aroma throughout the world, as they disclose the mysteries of the Trinity, the grace of Redemption, the largess of virtues, the glory of the Resurrection, and when his words explain the goal of eternal life. 'You have the words of eternal life', Peter says, 'to whom shall we go?'* Let us also say the same, anointed with his sweet perfume. In you, O good Jesus, breathes the Godhead of the Father who exists in you. In you breathes the grace of the Spirit who anointed you. In you breathes the virginity of your mother, in you the integrity of your own flesh, in you the healing of our languor. For us all these breathe their fragrant bouquet in you and to whom else shall we go either in love or in remembrance? Clearly wronged are such lilies, if any alien odor should mingle with them to make their perfume rank. Any malodor wafted to the nostrils of the spirit may corrupt it, turn it to the world, and make it hasten towards the stench of loathsome offal. Clearly it is wrong, if to you vices smell sweeter than lilies of virtues. He is squeamish indeed who does not delight to feed upon milk and among lilies. For not all milk is for babes. Does not all teaching, every devout affection gently poured into the spirit, seem to you to resemble milk? Whatever is easily and gently sipped, resembles milk.

5. With such milk the breasts of the bride were filled and so they are called 'like fawns', because in them the consolation of the word and an abundance of lively teaching is fresh and, as it were, ever new and reborn. These breasts know nothing of crabbed age and therefore they are better than wine,* yet not unlike must. 'Your breasts', says the Bridegroom,

Jn 6:69

Sg 1:1

'are like clusters of grapes',* having of course not the astringency of wine but the fresh sweetness of must. Other breasts feed; these intoxicate. Rightly then her breasts are like fawns, because they are not bruised by crabbed age. Great is the comeliness of the bust of the bride, if she has breasts unharmed, not a flabby bust crushed in the Egypt of this world.* That is why she said: 'My breasts are a tower.'* Unassailable are these breasts and teeming with plentiful milk, for they have grown up like a tower. Good then are breasts so distended, breasts of piety, twin breasts, for piety possesses the consolation both of the present life and of the life to come. Rejoice with great joy, says Isaiah, that you may have milk and be satisfied by the breasts of her consolation, and when you have been weaned from milk, you may feast from the entrance to her glory.* Do you see whither the use of milk leads? That you may feast, says Isaiah, from the entrance of her glory. Or do the breasts of the bride[3] not seem to you to feast from the entrance of glory, when like fawns 'they graze amid lilies until the day breaks and the shadows vanish'?* With what sweetness do breasts so nourished give suck, breasts filled from heaven because pastured among the lilies of heaven. The mere fragrance of lilies refreshes. Their perfume retains the flavor of food, for their perfume is fruit of a kind: 'like a vine', says Sirach, 'I yielded a fruit of sweet fragrance.'* See how wisdom counts her fragrance among fruits. This is food of the spirit, having nothing of the body, neither touched by the tooth nor chewed with difficulty, but breathed in by the spirit, flowing directly into the breasts themselves and expanding the breasts. For why are they said to be 'fragrant with the best ointments',* if not because in them the breath drawn from the neighboring lilies is fragrant, 'until the day breaks and the shadows vanish'.

6. It is delicious indeed amid lilies to await the rising dawn. Perhaps day is a neighbor of these lilies, and amid lilies often some wisp and mist of the day is inhaled. Even the Bridegroom himself grazes amid

Sg 7:7

Ezk 23:3, 21
Sg 8:10

Is 66:10-11, quoted loosely.

Sg 2:17, 4:5

Si 24:23

Sg 1:2

lilies, for he is himself the lily of the valleys and the light of day. It is delicious then in grazing with him to keep vigil for him, to be a sentinel amid the lilies until daylight breaks. That moment of which we speak, the psalmist indicates: 'I shall be content when your glory appears.'* Then the true and eternal day will break, when shadows vanish from the riddles through which we now see. Many are the shadows here: the shadow of delusion, the shadow of refreshment, the shadow of symbol. In the first slumbers the serpent, in the second the bride takes her rest, in the third the Bridegroom lies hidden. Of the first it is said: 'In shadow he slumbers';* of the second: 'I sat in the shadow of him whom I desired';* and of the third: Wisdom is hidden in mystery.* All these shadows will vanish before the breath of day: the shadow of deceit, the shadow of faith and the shadow of mystery. Then there will be no shadow, because truth will be naked. Then therefore will vanish the shadows which now loom high above us. Do you wish to know how high? 'Its shadow has covered the mountains.'*

A great mountain is Paul; yet he says he has been covered by this shadow for he sees only in a mirror and in riddles.* A great mountain, yet he is easily transported 'to the third heaven'.* It was a happy transport and much happier than the one by which the mountain in the Gospel, at the apostles' bidding, is cast into the sea.* A transport it was, because the wisdom of God changed Paul's perception. Therefore he was transported into the third heaven, the heaven of pure understanding, from which shadows and riddles have been exiled afar. Shadows are on a lower level and somehow fall short of the man transported to heaven. He was transported to heaven, transported also to paradise. Heaven is the realm of clear vision; paradise is the realm of pleasure. In a beautiful way Paul is transported to both, since contemplation which lacks either vision or pleasure is only half complete. In our text, the bride seems to be placed in some paradise of delights and pleasures, for she 'grazes amid lilies until the day breaks'.

Ps 16:15

Jb 40:16
Sg 2:3
1 Co 2:7

Ps 79:11

1 Co 13:12
2 Co 12:2

Mt 21:21

Before the day breaks, it is night. But this night seems to possess something of the day: 'Night', says the psalmist, 'is my illumination in my delights',[4] for delights to some extent take the place of illumination. It is a most beautiful realm for contemplation, where simple consideration of the faith sprinkles the dew of heavenly and fragrant affections and breathes in the grace of eternal light. These are not the delights which blessed Job mentions, when he says of wisdom, that 'it is not found in the land of those who live pleasantly'.* There is some share of wisdom in these delights. How is there not a share of wisdom where truth itself, though not yet fully understood but already believed, yields an agreeable flavor? Spiritual delights themselves, once experienced, teach sufficiently both how much what remains of them should be sought and how much whatever impedes them should be set at naught.*

    Jb 28:13

    Miquel, 153.

7. Three things should be noticed here: the time, the action and the place. The time, night-time, is a time of repose and freedom; the action is one of refreshment, because the fawns graze; the place is one of delight, because they graze amid lilies. With good reason does one return to babes with teeming breasts, when one so grazes, when one grazes in meditation on the faith, most freely, most fruitfully, most luxuriously. Do you think that 'Solomon in all his glory',* was clad as the bride who 'grazes amid the lilies'? How is she not gloriously clad, when she is cushioned with lilies? For although a shadow dims his beauty, she senses his perfume, senses the fragrance of his garments, and in these, as it were, she detects the fame of wisdom, 'until day breaks and the shadows vanish', that is until the day breaks, the day with no ending.

    Mt 6:29.
    Lam 183, n. 79.

As long as day and night alternate, shadows do not seem to vanish fully as long as they have a role to play. Where then have shadows disappeared? To be sure, with the Father of light, with whom there is no 'shadow of change'.* Every change bears the semblance of a shadow and while one change succeeds another, it hides and overshadows in some way the

    Jm 1:17

one which precedes. This then is the meaning of the words: 'until day breaks and the shadows vanish', that is, until the day breaks and high noon everlasting brings all shadows to an end. They 'who graze amid the lilies', says the Bridegroom, 'until day breaks and the shadows vanish', means those who relish and graze on the fragrance of wisdom, until the very brightness of eternal light dawns. In lilies, both qualities are praised, brightness and fragrance. Now what else is fragrance but the grace of faith; and what else is brightness but the glory of vision? By night fragrance is perceived, but brightness is not seen until daybreak, because brightness is the day itself with no share of shadows. When that day breaks, breasts will no longer be needed, for all will be taught by the day itself.* Meantime then the breasts of the bride are 'like two fawns . . . which graze amid lilies', until day breaks from the day, Christ Jesus.

NOTES ON SERMON TWENTY-SEVEN

1. Except for two references to his brethren, *Videtis, Fratres... Videtis,* in the first, and two in the fourth par., G. writes throughout to one individual. For the gazelle or wild goat, see Morson, 161-62, White 42-43.
2. Mab. and Migne: *verba (al. ubera)*; mss. Paris 9605, Troyes 419: *ubera*; the poet in G. conflates the two subjects, *ubera* and *verba* through the allusions in the rest of the sentence: *emollita sunt, qualia in Christo capere possunt,* since the words *emollita* and *parvuli* suggest the *lac parvulorum* of many texts, e.g. 1 Co 3:2, but *capere possunt* suggest Mt 19:11, *non omnes capiunt verbum istud.*
3. Ms Paris 9605: *sponsae*; Mab. and Migne: *sponsi.*
4. On 'consideration' see Lam 185, n. 97.

SERMON 28
THE INCENSE OF PRAYER

Purified, the lover's prayer rises like incense. 1. In community, one is refreshed by the perfumes of virtues. 2. The lilies of virtue are made inviolate by mortification. 3. Christ, anointed with myrrh, seeks the perfume of lilies on the mountain of myrrh. 4. At Christ's approach, He sets fire to our grains of incense. 5. Angels and saints pour out the incense of ardent prayer. 6-7. Prayer purifies the soul until it becomes like myrrh and incense.

I WILL GO TO THE MOUNTAIN OF MYRRH AND THE HILL OF FRANKINCENSE. YOU ARE ALL FAIR, MY LOVE; THERE IS NO FLAW IN YOU. COME WITH ME FROM LEBANON, MY BRIDE, COME WITH ME FROM LEBANON.*[1]   *Sg 4:6*

'Your breasts', says the Bridegroom, 'are like two fawns, twins of a gazelle'. You see how great is the charm of the bride; she is small and in her breasts like a young maiden. For what else does he mean but a young maiden, when he compares her breasts to fawns? Therefore she is both a mother and tiny, feeding others and needing to be fed. And if anyone be like Paul, still he has not yet given up childish ways, for he still dwells in the flesh.* Even though he has plenty for others, still he considers that he has not yet reached the goal.* He sees in a mirror, he sees in riddles;* then like a babe, like a fawn, he feeds in the

2 Co 13:11

Ph 3:13

1 Co 13:12

shadow until the day breaks. In the shadow he feeds but amid lilies.

Unhappy surely is the man who although placed amid the lilies, amid the lilies of a holy community, where on all sides various virtues yield their fragrance, has not learned to perceive any sweet perfume, anything resembling lilies. He is surely good and enjoys the bride's privilege, within whom are born these lilies of virtue, who feeds amid lilies, is refreshed amid lilies, hungers for lilies. For blessed are they who hunger and thirst for lilies of justice, lilies of chastity, lilies of all graces.* If it is blessed to hunger, it is much more blessed to feed amid lilies. Even hunger for virtues is itself nourishment and eagerness is a delight.* Fragrance is food but it does not yet satisfy. 'I shall be satisfied when your glory appears.'* In our text, the glory, as it were, of the virtues themselves is still hidden. All you perceive is their fragrance. Concealed is their beauty but we hear of their renown. Slight is the nourishment in renown, in smoke, in fragrance; sweet it is but slight. We also have already been satisfied, enriched, content with no more than the fragrance of virtues. Yet I wonder whether we have even breathed their fragrance, if eagerness for perfection does not allure us.

Sweet indeed is the scent of lilies but their sight is an added charm. Sweet indeed is the scent of lilies, but that sweetness is slight if it is nothing but perfume. Here the text says: 'who graze amid lilies', that is, 'in the midst of' but not 'upon' lilies, for they sense their proximity without enjoying their substance. A meager practice of virtues is expressed in fragrance, not a plentiful, solid and, as it were, a full-bodied repast. For one who grazes is not refreshed in full measure, so the text does not say 'those who are refreshed' but 'those who graze amid lilies until the day breaks'. Delightful, however, is the anticipation of light amid the lilies. Notice also the quality of the lilies where the bride grazes: amid lilies imperishable, lilies that never fester and lilies specifically spiced with the myrrh of incorruptibility, for myrrh means incorruption.*

Mt 5:6. Lam 13, n. 45

Ac 17:11
Ps 16:15

Sg 5:13

2. After the lilies rightly is added the verse about myrrh, to recommend to the bride lilies which endure without decay. 'I shall go', says the Bridegroom, 'for my own sake to the mountain of myrrh'.[2] Why is it, good Jesus, that your bride, your beloved, waits in one place while you go to another? Does she graze and wait amid the lilies while you go to the mountain of myrrh? Why do you not go rather to the lilies, where the bride lingers 'until the day breaks'? Or are these lilies perhaps no strangers to, nor planted far from, the mountain of myrrh, but instead arise upon it? Such is indeed the fact! Nowhere do lilies spring up more profusely than on a mountain of myrrh; nowhere are they better kept from harm. On a mountain of myrrh no place is left either for corruption or for corruptibility, there on the mountain of myrrh where all passions of the flesh are mortified, where lilies of chastity and lilies of the graces both spring up in purity and blossom unendingly.

So also you notice that both amid lilies and on the mountain of myrrh the bride has been placed pleasantly enough. For the present passage expresses the lilies for you; the myrrh you can express for yourself by interpretation. For how could the Bridegroom say he would go to a place other than that where he knew the beloved was? Indeed just as she is eagerly waiting, so is he ardently hastening. 'I will go', he says, 'for my own sake.' What then? Does he not go for the sake of the bride? Or does it follow that he goes only for his own sake because he goes towards the bride? 'I will go', then he says, 'for my own sake.' I will go for my own sake; not only for hers will I go. It is not she alone who derives joy from my arrival but to me no less does my arrival communicate her eagerness. Sweet to me, joyful to me, is my visit to her. I go now for my own sake. It profits me to go in this way; it causes me delight; therefore I go for my own sake. Now a sweet fragrance breathes for me from the mountain of myrrh; therefore I will go allured by the perfume. I will go for my own sake, because my delight is to tarry with the bride.

Is it so, good Jesus, that you take pleasure from

colloquy with the bride? So do you go for your own sake and unlike a disdainful lover do not turn aside when you are locked out but stand at the gate? You stand and knock and although you have suffered the insult of a rebuff, still you stand and knock, only that the door may be opened.* Sprinkle, O bride, sprinkle your chamber with myrrh and aloes.* Christ runs in the fragrance of your perfumes.* Sprinkle your chamber with the myrrh which Paul recalls: 'You have died and your life is hidden with Christ.'* With such myrrh sprinkle, water, drench your chamber or rather let your chamber become a mountain of myrrh. For grace abounds where myrrh grows more than where it is sprinkled. On this mountain set a chamber for your own sake or rather one for your Beloved in an abundance of myrrh, where this sweet-smelling plant is grown rather than imported.

Rv 3:20
Pr 7:17
Sg 1:3

Col 3:3

3. In many passages of Scripture myrrh is used to signify mysteries. With myrrh come the Magi to Christ;* 'Nicodemus also came bringing a mixture of myrrh, about a hundredweight.'* Here is a great supply, but what is it compared with a mountain? 'Bringing', says John, that is bringing with him, not producing from himself, shouldering it but not suffering it as Christ. Both are good, myrrh offered and myrrh grown, but the latter is better. In John the hundredweight is carried to Christ, but to this myrrh the Bridegroom goes himself. Indeed for his own sake he goes to the mountain of myrrh.

Mt 2:11
Jn 19:39

Well is he called a mountain of myrrh who bears within himself, not on his shoulder, the death of Christ,* not as if sprinkled with embalming myrrh but rich and solid and towering like a mountain of myrrh, and not for an hour and as if growing old but rather being born again.* Well is he called a mountain of myrrh who does not so much bear as beget in himself, as it were, Christ's death and incorruptibility and the image of his resurrection to come. Can he seem to you to be a mountain of myrrh, in whom appears none of the eminence, none of the loftiness of future incorruptibility, nothing but what is ephemeral? Blessed indeed is that mountain which is everywhere

2 Co 4:10

Rm 7:5; 9:2;
Ezk 17:22

covered with this full growth of myrrh, which is not dotted here and there with a patchwork of these plants, which has no bare spots, no barren ground but is wholly fertile with this blessed plant.

How is that mountain not blessed which draws Christ to it in the fragrance of its aromatic perfume? Good is that fragrance which fills not only the house of the leper* but also the palace of heaven, the chamber of the Bridegroom. Good is that fragrance surely, for it is pleasing to Christ the Bridegroom even amid the delights of his Godhead. In our text, beyond such delights, his delight is to be upon the mountain of myrrh. Hence he says: 'I will go' for my own sake 'to the mountain of myrrh.' *Mt 26:6-7*

4. O blessed mountain to which you go, good Jesus, to which you come, over which you range, on which you dwell and will dwell to the end,* on which you alone dwell and that to its utmost bounds. Come, Jesus, begin to possess this mountain. Let no one introduce an inquiry about you; let no one say: are you to dwell on this mountain alone? A fertile mountain, a prolific mountain, a mountain abounding, a mountain overflowing with spices! These spices cannot be exhausted. Great indeed is the store of spices on the mountain of myrrh. Spices will not disappear from this mountain; therefore he who goes to the mountain of myrrh will not want for spices; he will not even lack perfumes who goes to the hills of Lebanon. *Ps 36:29*

Frankincense will not disappear from Lebanon. For the name Lebanon, they say, means incense. Come to these hills, good Jesus, that incense may flow before the fire of your countenance. O what a cloud of incense rises from these hills, when they are kindled by your fire or rather by you who are the fire! Your fire has plenteous fuel on the hills of incense and abundant tinder. These grains are not quickly consumed; the clouds from this incense do not easily disappear. Such a store, such plenty from the hill of incense cannot be grasped in a fist or contained in a thurible; it is not stored in a bin; it knows no measure because its flow knows no interruption.

Rightly therefore is he a hill of incense who prays without ceasing,* and what is more satisfying, without slackening, who in prayer has nothing lax, nothing meager but as the smoke from some great forge billows forth, so he emits columns of billowing aspirations and outpouring desires. Come then, good Jesus, to the hills of incense; the mountains you touch pour columns of smoke rich with the incense of prayer. What have our prayers, brothers, comparable to this? How quickly our incense becomes stale! And somehow it hardly catches fire before it goes out. Why is this? Undoubtedly because we have collected for ourselves but a meager stock of incense.

1 Th 5:17

5. For my part I consider as hills of incense the angelic spirits and among men any who seek to rival the angels, for their prayer like incense always rises in the sight of God;* they generate most fragrant clouds of devotion; from them billow cloud-racks of heavenly affections. Blessed certainly is the priest who offers so much incense that a veil of incense so fragrant serves as his cloak and his cape. In the Apocalypse you read of 'bowls full of incense which are the prayers of the saints'.* And what is the relationship between hills and bowls of incense? For what bowl could contain a hill of incense? Good is a bowl full of incense. But see something more than a bowl is here. 'The smoke of incense rose', says the text, 'from the hand of the angel' in the sight of the Lord.*

Ps 140:2

Rv 5:8

Rv 8:4

But what hand can match a whole hill? What hand, I ask, but your hand, good Jesus. For you weigh the mountains and enclose the earth in your palm, you 'weigh the mountains on scales, the hills in a balance'.* In your hand, O Lord, are all the bounds of these hills and, if we may say so, in your bosom. In the text, it is to your bosom that the prayer of the saints is turned.* It enters into your sight;* there it dwells; there it is changed; those who pray are in you and you are in them. Consequently 'I will go for my own sake', you say, 'to the hills of incense'. Come then, Lord; come and tarry not; come and do not leap beyond these hills. What if the hills of

Is 40:12

Ps 34:13
Rv 8:4

incense also leap towards you? Mobile are the mountains of myrrh and the hills of incense, when you approach. How are they not mobile, when they melt, flow, billow, ascend from your hand like the smoke of incense in the sight of the Lord? Go then for your own sake to the hills of incense, where incense is plentiful, where everything is incense, for on the hill of incense nothing exists without incense. This incense has been given for your sake; come then to burn it in your sight.

6. 'I will go' for my sake 'to the mountain of myrrh and to the hill of incense. Come from Lebanon, come.' The reason for his going has already been deduced; what is it but to invite, to enter and to say 'Come'? 'Behold how good and how pleasant it is'* to dwell on these hills to which the Word of God goes, which he revisits, from which he invites the bride and invites her to a crown!* 'Come from Lebanon', he says, 'come, you shall be crowned!' Lebanon means 'whiteness'. What else but white with snow from heaven? For snow, says Jeremiah, shall not depart from Lebanon.* That is snow which falls from heaven, which drifts over the land, inebriates it and makes it germinate. Blessed are the mountains upon which this snow falls and the hills it covers. 'So shall it be', says the Lord, 'with the word which issues from my mouth; it will not return to me empty.'*

Ps 132:1

Sg 4:8

Jr 18:14

Is 55:11

Does the word seem to you to return empty which goes to the mountains of myrrh and the hills of incense, which falls upon these mountains and covers these hills? It knows not how to return empty. Therefore he invites and says: 'Come from Lebanon, come!' Or do you think the text has no hidden meaning when after the mountains of myrrh and the hills of incense the text mentions Lebanon? What makes the spirit so clean and so white as the practice of prayer? First indeed myrrh mortifies, then incense purifies. For prayer will be unable to rise without impurity, unless every malodor and stench of the flesh has first been banned. In the anointing of myrrh, the mind pulls itself together to concentrate into some, indeed into total, unity; by the burning of incense, the mind is guided and opened and pours itself out and fills the heavenly realms with the fragrance of incense. There it blends and flows into the free breath of truth and the soul which at first was bound up in itself there becomes subtle, refined and faint, hanging in air and looking on high.*

Lam 188-89, nn. 123, 124.

7. Prayer fulfils the function of both myrrh and incense. First it gathers and binds together into yourself your affections when you pray; then it releases them to transmit them to God. What is more like myrrh, when there is such an outpouring towards union with God? What is more like incense, when there is such an effusion towards some perception of God? Rightly is the bride called all fair and flawless, when the ardor of prayer makes her incandescent, when the brightness of eternal light dyes her with its color and makes her radiant.*

Lam 189, nn. 123-126; 190, n. 132.

'You are all fair, my love; there is no flaw in you.' 'You are all fair', because you are wholly beautiful, especially at this hour, the hour of prayer, the hour of incense. 'You are all fair my love, you are all fair', because you are wholly beloved and incandescent with the sole affection of love. 'You are all fair and without flaw', having no admixture of alien hue. 'Come from Lebanon; come from Lebanon, come from Lebanon!' 'Come from Lebanon' because you are without flaw; 'come from Lebanon', because you are all fair!' 'Come from Lebanon', because you are fully cleansed. 'Come from Lebanon', wholly enlightened; 'come from Lebanon', free from fault; 'come from Lebanon' bright with grace; 'come, you shall wear the crown'.

Utterly happy is one who from the Lebanon of bright affection, from the hill of incense, from abundance of intense prayer, is called to a crown. Happy is the soul, I say, which at the hour of incense rises to the Father, which without interval is called from Lebanon to a crown, the crown of glory, with which at the hour of passover he will reward the soul, her just Judge and sweet Spouse, Jesus Christ with God the Father for ever and ever. Amen.

NOTES TO SERMON TWENTY-EIGHT

1.   G. seems to write for one individual: *vide* in par. 1, *advertis* in par. 2, *Orantis . . . in te ipsum* in par. 7; however he adapts for his brethren: *Videtis* in par. 1, and *fratres . . . nostrae . . . nostra . . .* at the end of par. 4.

2.   '*Vadam*', *inquit*, '*mihi ad montem myrrhae*'; Vulg. omits '*mihi*'.

SERMON 29
INVITED TO A CROWN

The beloved is invited from Lebanon to a crown. 1. The triple call is a sign of passionate love for the bride's beauty. 2. At the hour of prayer, the soul is all fair. 3. The power of love is supreme. 4. Tribulation is preparation for a crown. 5. The bride is called to the conversion of the Gentiles. 6. From Lebanon she brings mountainous peoples to Lebanon. 7. In communities such people are found, not to the Bride's despair but to her glory. 8. The bride's example is to be imitated by those who assume office.

WHOLLY BEAUTIFUL ARE YOU, MY LOVE, AND WITHOUT BLEMISH. COME FROM LEBANON, MY BRIDE; COME FROM LEBANON. COME, YOU SHALL WEAR THE CROWN; COME FROM THE PEAK OF AMANA AND THE CRESTS OF SENIR AND HERMON, FROM THE LAIRS OF LIONS AND THE MOUNTAINS OF LEOPARDS.*[1]   *Sg 4:7-8*

Wholly beautiful are you, my love, and without blemish. Come from Lebanon, Come, you shall wear the crown.' Who will grant me to complete, as it were, 'this journey of three days'?* Who, I ask, will grant me to travel this road with unwearied step? 'These roads are beautiful roads and these are paths of peace',* to come from Lebanon to Lebanon, from Lebanon to a kingdom. For the bride called to a

*Gn 30:36;
Jon 3:3*

Pr 3:17

crown seems invited to share in the kingship. Delightful is this end of the road but no less delightful is the journey. How could the road fail to delight, since it knows no detour from Lebanon? This is no broad way, this is no worldly way; neither can 'anyone defiled pass along it'.* It depends neither on man's speed nor on his will but on the mercy of God.* Why do I say mercy? I might have done better to say God's longing. Does his triple call not express the avowal of ardent longing? That he calls a third time is a proof of his passionate affection.

 Review in your mind earlier verses of this Canticle. Nowhere will you find the beauty of the bride so often invoked or so explicitly acclaimed. Three times he calls, saying she is wholly beautiful. In earlier verses of the Song you will find: 'Behold, you are beautiful, my love. Behold, you are beautiful', and again later: 'Oh how beautiful you are, my love! how beautiful you are!'* But in this third place he proclaims her 'wholly beautiful'. In the earlier verses, he either shows that she is beautiful or marvels that she is so beautiful; he does not, however, avow precisely that she is wholly beautiful as in the present verse: 'You are wholly beautiful, my love.' How is she not wholly beautiful, when she is compared with beauty and wholly compared with all beauty? How is she not wholly beautiful, when into her flows the limitless brightness of eternal light?* Truly she is wholly beautiful and surpassing beautiful, when into her at full tide pours all the beauty of the Lord. Yes, his beauty is exalted above the stars but the mirror of his beauty is in his bride. His mirror, we read, is in the clouds of heaven.* As long as the bride is a cloud of heaven, a cloud bright and airy, as it were, approaching and enfolding the Sun, so long does the splendor only of the Sun reflect in her and she remains the mirror of his beauty.

 2. Clearly then the bride is a cloud because she enjoys the lightness of spiritual affection and the light of understanding. As long as the spiritual soul by the practice of prayer and contemplation is poised on high like a bright and airy cloud, it is all the

while wholly beautiful because it is wholly beloved, and without blemish because it has been changed into the color of fervent charity. At the hour of prayer the Bridegroom 'presents the bride to himself in splendor without blemish or wrinkle',* cleansing her not so much in his Blood as in his light. How is she not wholly beautiful, in whom the splendor of divine beauty is so clearly expressed? *Eph 5:27*

What soul will you show me, which you would dare to define as wholly beautiful, save at this hour alone, when by the ardor of love it is rather dyed than robed in the splendor of the Bridegroom? At other times indeed the soul is reputed to be without blemish when no fault is imputed. But at this moment the remark that she is without blemish comes not from indulgence but from love, from longing and from devotion. What place is there for pardon where the aspirations of charity are so ardent? Love needs no indulgence, for everything is full of grace where there is love and love alone. In our text now notice how both offence is excluded and grace is commended, grace alone. 'Wholly beautiful are you, my love', he says, 'and without blemish.' Compliments of this kind seem characteristic not of one who shows indulgence but of one who is enamored, who is full of love and admiration. Allured by her beauty, he desires her presence, 'Come from Lebanon; come from Lebanon, come, you shall wear the crown.' The repeated invitation betrays his affection, manifests his longings.

3. Let others search for the hidden meaning of the triple call and determine its degrees; for me it is enough to marvel at the affection of the divine Majesty for the human soul. This is enough but it is quite beyond me. Would that I had nothing to do but to wonder at the grace bestowed, ever rapt in amazement, yet so that my aspirations might match my wonder and my love go hand in hand. For affection deserves affection and deep calls to matching deep in the roar of tumbling waterfalls.* Good are the waterfalls which pour forth your affection, good Jesus, and instil your love. *Ps 41:8*

Love is not mute; it has a voice to use, for 'that

which holds all things together has knowledge of the voice'.* This verse is written of the Spirit and you are well aware what kinship, if not rather what identity, exists between charity and the Spirit. Charity holds all together because charity is the fulfilment of the law.² The Spirit speaks mysteries and openly speaks the mysteries of love.³ The Spirit himself bears witness to our spirit,* yes, and can pay a compliment. The sound he makes is a feeling of love and longing and has sighs like a voice. The very experience of grace is certainly the fact that he speaks, that he invites, that he calls, 'Come from Lebanon'.

He calls three times perhaps precisely because 'a cable of three strands is difficult to break'.* A tenacious cable indeed is love. Love lures by affection. For love, to chat is to charm. Nothing is more tenacious than the bond of love; nothing is more alluring. Hear how the law of God proclaims the triple twining of this cable: 'You shall love the Lord your God with all your heart and all your soul and all your mind'*—as if to say: you shall love the Lord your God with the resolve of your heart, with the living affection of your soul, with some full and rational decision of your mind, that there may exist in you a resolution to love which itself is determined and discerning.

Good of course is an intention of the heart devoted to God, but what if your intention be sluggish, devoid of vitality and spirit? Good then is a pure intention which fervent and tender affection makes lively and spirited. This affection, which is like the soul of a good resolution, meditation informs if it is discreet and fosters if it is frequent. What is richer for meriting the crown kept in reserve than this cable of triple ply?* What better designed to anticipate the crown by experience? Does this triple love not seem to you to invite as it were to call three times: 'Come'?

4. In our text the Bridegroom invites, as it were, while he bestows both the boldness to merit and the eagerness to experience the crown. 'Come from Lebanon'; he calls. 'Come, you shall wear the crown.'

In the Apocalypse you read, as it were, of those coming from Lebanon: 'Who are these, clothed in white robes, and whence have they come? . . . These are they who have come out of great tribulation and have washed their robes and bleached them in the blood of the Lamb.'* 'They have bleached their robes in the blood of the Lamb', yes, both by the loyalty of their faith and by their way of life, for in their tribulation they follow this Lamb, who did not open his mouth when he was being led to slaughter and was dumb before his shearer.* They are not downcast or rebellious until they exchange judgment for victory* and a contest for a crown, for only he will be crowned who observes the rules of the contest.*

Rv 7:13-14

Is 53:7

Is 42:4; Mt 12:20

2 Tm 2:5. Reading donec for quamdiu with Mab.

Because the crown is the issue of the contest, perhaps he invites his beloved to a crown in such a way as to express its reason, for he says: 'You shall be crowned from the peaks of Amana and Senir, from the mountains of leopards, from the lairs of lions.'* Something rugged, something wild, something crafty is conveyed by their names or by their natures. So the bride is said to be crowned after these, because her triumph over them provides the reason for the crown. For through endurance of tribulation he is crowned who from great tribulation comes meek, gentle and like a lamb,* who in the fire of charity comes incandescent but not consumed,* not charred by any soot of impatience or complaint.* These are they who come from Lebanon and are crowned 'from the peaks of Amana and Senir, from the lairs of lions, from the mountains of leopards'. Through these trials indeed they are crowned, who are tested by trials of these kinds. Do they not gather 'grapes from thorns and figs from brambles'?* 'This slight momentary affliction', says the apostle, 'is preparing for us an eternal weight of glory beyond all comparison.'* The sufferings of the present time', then, prepare for but do not compare with the future crown of glory reserved for us.* Obviously matter for reward accumulates, when amid the merits of full integrity one is chastened by various

Sg 4:8

Jer 11:19
Heb 12:29

Jdt 8:24; 25.
Lam 16, n. 64.

Mt 7:16

2 Co 4:17

Rm 8:18

sufferings. Most beautiful is the welding of the crown, when purity of life and humble endurance of oppression cling together.

Great indeed is the weight of oppression, so perhaps it has been expressed by the names of mountains. Massive is their bulk, but faith incapable of being overwhelmed rises above their bulk. Faith sets its heel on the peaks of those mountains and strikes the very 'peak from the house of the godless'.* Rightly therefore is the head itself crowned for it triumphs over the head, because it both crushes the beginning of temptations and does not yield to the violence of tribulations. In everything, that is, like the head, which is either the first or the greatest. So here take 'head' as if you were allowed to understand either the source or the summit of the things symbolized by these mountains. From the peak of Amana, from the summit of Hermon and Senir, he is crowned who has risen above an accumulation of wrongs and a mass of tribulations which tower aloft against the humble knowledge of Christ.* But this mass seems to have the less weight, the more everything inflated is transitory.

5. In our text, although the mass is a mountain, yet you find it written that 'the mountain falls and crumbles and the rock is removed from its place'.* And see how these mountains have crumbled, how these mountains have been removed. They have been removed because they have been changed. The apostle shows that people, like mountains, were moved and vanquished, for he says to them: 'Such were some of you' once 'but you were washed, you were sanctified, you were justified',* by this washing and cleansing which is brought about by the word of faith. The 'pard' has been stripped of his stripes,[4] been made wholly without blemish, wholly of one color, that is, of one faith and one way of life. Like the 'pard' indeed seems the man who has been painted with stripes of heretical dogma and no less like the 'pard' is the man who is unlike himself, wavering and inconstant and suddenly changing his plans. For the 'pard', so to speak, wills and wills not.*

Apply this to the conversion of the Gentiles and you will understand at once how, by unity of faith and hope, those who have been converted to the Lord seem to have put on one color. They stripped off, you will notice, not only their alternating stripes, but also their wildness; they dwell not in the lairs of lions, 'not in lairs of debauchery and licentiousness', I mean,* but in lairs and gardens of perfume;† they rest not in beds of wild beasts, not in beds defiled but in beds of flowers. For the bed of the bride and Bridegroom is all flowers.* The bride does not seem to depart willingly from Lebanon and from Judah to pass over to the Gentiles. For she leaves reluctantly; though called so often, she is loth to abandon Lebanon in order to pass over to Mount Amana, to the peaks of Senir and Hermon. But by her passing she changes these barren mountains, these barbarous mountains, into a Lebanon.

*Rm 13:13
†Sg 4:16

Sg 1:15

6. Now examine the names of these mountains. Amana means a 'vain' or a 'confining' people. Senir means 'shaggy'. Hermon means 'anathema'. What more vain than that people whose very teachers 'made nonsense of logic' and 'claiming to be philosophers, became fools'?* What more confining than they who in despair surrendered to impurity?* Confined indeed is the heart which limits the range of its longings to the goals of temporal enjoyment, not knowing how to expand its hope to things eternal.* What could be more shaggy and unkempt than they whom the apostle calls 'heartless, implacable, motivated by malice and envy'?* Are these not to be reckoned as Senir? For Hermon means those who are strangers to the understanding of Christ, having no hope of the promise,* not 'fellow citizens of the saints', not 'belonging to God's household', but altogether 'without God in this world'.* And this indeed, O Gentiles, you were, but 'you have been washed, sanctified and justified in the name of our Lord Jesus'* and therefore from you the bride is crowned for she glories in your transformation. Good is that transformation by which Senir is changed into Lebanon.

Rm 1:21-22
Rm 1:24

2 Co 6:11

2 Tm 3:3; Tt 3:3

Eph 2:12

Eph 2:19;
Eph 2:12.

1 Co 6:11

But Lebanon indeed, that earlier Jewish Lebanon, now seems to be changed into Senir and Hermon. Therefore, 'come from Lebanon', come and see, in place of that lowly and short-lived Lebanon, how many Lebanons rise in your honor. 'Lift up your eyes round about and see',* in your honor all the mountains of this world must be changed into Lebanon. It is obviously painful to see the losses and desolation of your nation, but this pain is compensated for by an exchange so profitable that the losses of one are redeemed by a more abundant profit from many.⁵ Do not add delay to delay then, but come from a Lebanon which now ceases to be Lebanon. Come that you may be crowned for the faith and the conversion of the Gentiles. Do you wish to interpret all these mountains not as in Judea and among the Gentiles, but only in the Church? This will not be a discordant interpretation, if you choose to understand the matter in this sense. You will find here a Lebanon and an Amana, a Senir and a Hermon. You will find here mountains of 'pards' and lairs of lions.

Is 49:18

7. Would that in this Lebanon of ours in this holy community of monks, which both our profession and our way of life make charming and chaste, in our Lebanon, I say, would that one could discern neither the peak of Amana nor the crests of Senir and Hermon. When you see in an assembly and congregation of saints someone exalting himself, puffed up with the wisdom of the flesh,* vain in his boasting, interiorly and exteriorly irascible and cantankerous, fretful in the emptiness of idleness—for idleness breeds frustration—when you see such a man, what else are you discerning but the peak of Amana with Lebanon? Nothing is more empty than idleness, nothing more fretful than frustration,* nothing more cantankerous than irascibility.⁶ For Amana also means a 'vain' or 'fretful' people; therefore from Amana one comes to Senir, to a shaggy and hairy race.

Col 2:18. Lam 13, n. 46; 18, n. 73.

acedia

For where there is frustration, there is irascibility. Where there is cantankerousness, there is nothing gentle, nothing composed, nothing orderly, but everything bristles and someone of such a character is devoid of tact, without affection, full of hostility and disaffection,* indeed anathematized, which is the meaning of Mount Hermon. Such a man is not of God's household, not a fellow citizen, not even a resident alien or a guest,* and therefore no grace, no devotion pays him a visit. The Bridegroom does not turn aside to visit him even in passing or stay with him as a guest. But there dwell with him 'pards', demons of striped and turncoat hides, and with him lions make their lairs. They do not go out of their way to hasten past but hold him fast and bed down with him. But such characters should not be given up in despair, for many of this sort are predestined to be ornaments of the Bridegroom. Therefore he says: 'Come, you shall be crowned from the peak of Amana and from the crest of Senir.' 'Come', he says, 'from Lebanon come.' *Rm 1:31; Col 1:21* *Eph 2:19*

Consider whether the bride drags her feet in coming from Lebanon, for she is called so often. Yet her delay is caused not by contumacy but by caution. For who is eager to depart from the brightness of contemplation and from the serenity of inner repose and purity?[7] To whom will it not be painful to withdraw even for a moment from a place of delights? Perhaps the gains expected amid disciples are attractive but the labor is painful. Though gains are desirable, still a fall is to be feared. I am suspicious of gains when their outcome is uncertain, when danger to my own salvation is imminent and the loss of interior delight is certain. Why wonder if the bride delays in coming, since it is both painful to leave Lebanon and fearful to approach those barbaric mountains, the haunts of wild beasts? And perhaps the bride's delay is a blow and a reproach to our haste, for with excessive readiness and little forethought, not weighing our capacities, we hasten to enter upon the labors of authority, upon the pains of anxious care and upon an occasion to stumble. Not even awaiting the first invitation, as volunteers we seize office for ourselves, either anticipating a call or securing one by manipulation. When the charge is so great, there should be neither heedless presumption nor again obstinate fear.

8. In the light of our text, we may presume to accept when Christ orders, when the Bridegroom calls and promises abundant rewards, as in the present verse: 'Come, you shall be crowned from the peak of Amana, from the crests of Senir and Hermon, from the lairs of lions, from the mountains of "pards".' When subjects lay aside the barbarity of their behavior, when from their lairs of 'debauchery and licentiousness' they move to flower-decked and honest lodgings and to gardens of perfumes, to lodgings in which there are not growls but tears, to lodgings in which there is not a battle of wits but compunction of heart, when the cloak of blemished stripes is removed and naked simplicity takes its place, when behavior has been changed for the better by her ministry, then understandably the bride is being welcomed for her crown. Fairly indeed is she crowned thanks to such characters, for they now are changed into an adornment though previously she abhorred their behavior and now, as it were, in the ranks of charity they cling together in unity, though previously they dwelt apart in disagreement, red in tooth and claw.

Pleasing surely to the Bridegroom is this fellowship in unity; perhaps this is why he proceeds to say he has been 'wounded by one of her eyes, by one hair of her neck', because, of course, she is his bride. The explanation of this verse must be postponed to another time. But it will be enough to give this advice in conclusion, that if care for the progress of others entices anyone to seek a higher rank, I do not dissuade him, as of course I do not persuade him. One thought however I do urge upon you, whoever you are with such a problem, that you emulate both the delay and the purity of the bride, who is not content to be called once or worthy to be called at all, except from the Lebanon of a pure and snow-white conscience, for only from Lebanon does Christ Jesus her Bridegroom call his beloved to a crown, for he is God, blessed for ever and ever. Amen.

NOTES ON SERMON TWENTY-NINE

1. G. addresses one person throughout.
2. Rm 13:10. Lam quotes Gregory the Great, *Hom. 30 in Ev.* 1; PL 76: 1220B: *Ipse Spiritus sanctus Amor est.* See F. Vandenbrouke, 'L'action du Saint-Esprit dans les âmes', *DSp* 4 (1961) 1309-10; P. Smulders, 'Saint Augustin: le Saint-Esprit Charité', *DSp* 4 (1961) 1279-1283; J.M. Déchanet, *Aux sources de la spiritualité de Guillaume de Saint-Thierry* (Bruges, 1940) 17 n. 4.
3. 1 Co 14:2; and for *amatoria* see Seneca, *Ep Mor.* 9:6, 'Hecato says, "I can show you a philtre, *amatorium,* compounded without drugs, herbs, or any witch's incantations; if you would be loved, love, *si vis amari, ama"*.' Interestingly the first two words in Gilbert are also found in this epistle: 'the affections of lovers, *affectus amantium*', 9:11, SC 1:1.
4. Gilbert's *pardus* is striped like a tiger not spotted like a leopard. See Morson, pp. 152-4, White, 13-14.
5. See G. Ep 1:2, where G. talks of recouping one's losses and uses the language of Seneca, *Ep Mor.* 81:1.
6. Frustration = *acedia;* for the verb *acedior* see Si 6:26; 22:16; Migne, mss Paris 9605, Troyes 419: *tumore;* Mab: *timore.* Lam 196, n. 174.
7. See Leclercq, 'Otia Monastica,' 119:21.

SERMON 30
UNION OF MINDS AND HEARTS

The lover longs for union of minds and hearts. 1. The heart of the Bridegroom is wounded with love; our love cannot repay his spendthrift love. 2. Affectionate love wounds the heart of Jesus; every affectionate glance is a wounding dart. 3. The eye is a pure intention and the hair is attentive meditation. 4. Join orderly meditation on Scripture to unity of intention. 5. Her locks are believers in unity and community. 6. The rending of her locks by schism wounds the heart of her Beloved. 7. Divine Providence and human devotedness are two sides of the same seal. 8. For unity, bishops are deprived of temporal possessions; for temporal possessions, the Pope is less severe towards schismatics. 9. Jesus allows no middle course, but when will he remove the gall and pour oil into her wounds?

YOU HAVE WOUNDED MY HEART, SISTER, MY BRIDE, YOU HAVE WOUNDED MY HEART, WITH ONE OF YOUR EYES AND ONE HAIR OF YOUR NECK.*[1] *Sg 4:9*

O hard heart, O heart obstinately hard, if in you these words do not beget wounds! Insensate indeed is the heart which does not feel deeply the force of these words, which is not amazed at so much graciousness.* Why do I say 'graciousness'? It is even more. Yet how *Sr 32:3* great it would be, if it were merely graciousness! Great indeed were the deed and full worthy of wonder, if such Majesty merely bowed to grace human infirmity with the titles of 'sister' and 'bride'. In reality, however, it is not so much graciousness as devotedness. But do you wish to hear the proof of his avowed and prodigal affection? 'You have wounded my heart', he says, 'sister, my bride, you have wounded my heart.'

The wound in his heart denotes the vehemence of his love. O heart truly tender, moved by such affection for us as to seek an exchange of love for love! This is at once a relationship and an exchange; the relationship is indicated by the titles sister and bride; the exchange by the wound. Close is the relationship of a sister, that of a bride even closer; the former is one of kinship, the latter one of love. Sister indicates a unity of origin, but bride indicates union. The bride is a sister because she shares the nature God assumed, but she is a bride because she has been assumed into the uniqueness of his person. These titles obviously express a relationship, for they refer either to nature or to grace. How much should she love, when she knows she is covenanted with Christ by such close kinship!

However much she loves, she does not simply love but she returns love for love. In fact he first loved us.* However prodigally our love for him is spent, it is not so much paid as repaid; it is a debt not a benefaction. It cannot match the love already expended. And how can our love earn or deserve a return, when it is not sufficient to repay in full? No, O bride, you cannot make a full payment in return to your Beloved! Yet he does not stop squandering his love. What he spends on you has not yet been fully repaid and yet he feels under an obligation. Whatever love you repay him, he does not receive as a debt but as a benefaction. He feels deeply that he has been, as it were, challenged to love, when he confesses that his heart has been wounded.[2]

2. What marvel is this, brothers? Do you not regard this soul as blessed which pierces and penetrates

1 Jn 4:10

the very heart of our Lord Jesus Christ by its devout affections? Sharp and effective and truly violent is the affection, good Jesus, which woos and wins your affection! Strong and violent is the force of charity which reaches and penetrates the very affection of God and like an arrow transfixes his vital organs.* *Pr 7:23* What wonder if 'the kingdom of heaven suffers violence'!* The Lord himself bears the wound of *Mt 11:12* violent love.

But see by what shafts he is wounded. 'You have wounded my heart', he says, 'with one of your eyes and with one hair of your neck.' Do not hesitate, O bride, to aim such weapons at your Spouse. Use devout glances as darts. Do not act too remissly in the engagement;* do not be content to wound your *2 M 12:14* Beloved once but pierce him with wound after wound.* Happy are you if your arrows are fixed in *Jb 16:15* him* and your shafts of love do battle in Christ, if *Ps 37:3* your eye is fixed upon him unwearyingly. Good is the wound from which power issues. A woman touched his hem and Christ felt power go forth from him.* *Lk 8:43-46* When his heart is not lightly touched but is wounded, how much more does he feel grace flow from himself? This wound does not pass unfelt; therefore aim at him the arrows of a pure gaze; regard him as a target set up for such arrows.

Such he welcomes with favor, for such are the arrows he fires. He glanced at Peter, struck his heart and pierced him to repentance.* Tears give signs of a *Lk 22:61-62* wounded heart. In that text, with a look of clemency, he wounds that heart which he moves to some affection for virtue. May he multiply such wounds in me, from the sole of my foot to the crown of my head, that there may be no soundness in me!* For no sound health is there where there are *Is 1:6* no wounds inflicted by the loving gaze of Christ. One gaze challenges another; therefore try to wound him with your view from afar. Let your eyes be ever upon the Lord,* that he may be captured in the glances of *Ps 24:15* your love,* that he may be ensnared in your curls. *Is 3:16*

3. Yet he does not say 'with your eyes' or 'with your hair' in the plural, but in the singular; 'You

have wounded my heart, sister, my bride, you have wounded my heart with one of your eyes and with one hair of your neck.' If you have several eyes, shut all others, that you may rely on that one only with which you are wont and able to gaze upon the Beloved. Those who want a sharper view, cock one eye, fix the other on the object and focus the open eye for a more reliable view in a direct line. Your eye is one if it is pure; it is one if it is not directed to many objects; it is one if somehow it is simplified and focused upon and directed to one object, not split, not wandering, not divided among many objects. Your eye is one if you always view and focus on one object and on that alone. In our text, if it is the eye of love, it is one. 'One thing I have asked of the Lord', says the psalmist, 'this will I implore, that I may dwell in the house of the Lord all the days of my life, that I may behold the beauty of the Lord.'* His eye was one, for it sought one object and looked to one alone.

Ps 26:4. Lam 184, nn. 93, 94.

'And with a hair of your neck.' It is not becoming that locks should stray like lawless vagabonds and tramps in disarray, brushing against the eyes. It is not right that while the eye is fixed, the hair should be disheveled. For the eye is impeded when the hair floats free. If the eye is taken to mean the intention, what does the hair denote but thought? Would you have each of the two together; eyes and hair, intention and meditation? The man 'whose will is fixed on the law of the Lord and who meditates on it day and night',* also possesses an eye at one in a consistent resolution and hair at one in meditation. Otherwise if your attention to God is not consistent and simple, if your thoughts stray uncontrolled, the antics of a wandering and undisciplined mind stun the eye trying to focus, shock the direct line of vision from its purpose and shatter the heart. Let pure intention have corresponding thought, thought that is one, just as the intention is consistent. For good is the hair which is not scraggly, not unkempt, but gathered into one and clinging to the neck, yes, the neck of which it is said: Your neck is like a tower, from which hang

Ps 1:2

a thousand shields.*   *Sg 4:4. Lam 179, n. 53.*

4. Interpret this neck as sacred Scripture, through which words flow to us, words which announce the divine will. Consistently then a hair of the neck is interpreted as assiduous thought on the law of God. So it is said to be 'of the neck' because all your thought, all your interpretations and all your understanding must not forestall God's word, but depend on and progress from its direction. If, however, your locks be divided and, as it were, torn and in total disarray, though they cling to the neck, they neither please the bridegroom nor wound his heart; they neither stir his affection nor merit his grace.

He makes two demands: that your locks be united and kept close to your neck, that they display both good order and authority. For what does it profit you, if your meditations are upon the law of God, if in themselves they are lawless? Thoughts are lawless if they are without order and become the sport of the winds. 'With one hair of your neck', says the Bridegroom. By the neck is understood the authority of the sacred word, for it shapes our thoughts; but by the unity of the hair is understood order. Now that order is good, where the locks are gathered together and brought into unity and into a unity which is not taken away.* Or the Bridegroom says, 'with one hair of your neck' precisely to indicate that the face of the bride is free and unveiled, for hair is regarded as a veil.* The Bridegroom then wants in the bride a face without mask or veil to view the glory of God and to fix the eye of contemplation without impediment; so he commends well-ordered locks drawn back from the countenance to the nape of the neck.

Lk 10:42

1 Co 11:15

5. Why are we applying this to one soul individually? Let us extend our interpretation to the condition of the Church. For more pleasant is what applies in common. In Scripture nothing is more pleasing to the Bridegroom than the community, or rather the unity of believers[3] and the embrace of the Church. He gathered many qualities to eulogize his bride and by them showed his pleasure, but never has he expressed the emotion of shared joy so much as

here, where the unity of both eye and hair[4] is called to mind. How will his joy not be greatest where the greatest commandment is observed? 'A new commandment I give you', he says, 'that you love one another as I have loved you.'*

Jn 13:34

The eyes of the Church are its doctors and he who touches them touches the pupil of the eye of the Lord. But its locks are the peoples who believe. In each of the two is a unity pleasing to the Bridegroom. 'By this', he says, 'all men will know that you are my disciples, if you have love for one another.'* The accord of two or three makes their prayers achieve their goal;* how much more the accord of the whole Church in Christ? How does unity not achieve its goal when it penetrates the very heart of the Lord? 'You have wounded my heart, sister, my bride, you have wounded my heart with one of your eyes and one hair of your neck.' For of all feminine adornment what more allures and moves the affection of a lover than hair well dressed?* But why are we trying to heap praises on the hair of the bride, combed and arranged with winning gracefulness? Here lies an ample subject for elegy rather than for eulogy.

Jn 13:35

Mt 18:20

1 Co 11:15, Si 26:21.

6. In our day we see the locks of the bride pitifully torn out and cut off and the peoples of the Church fighting among themselves for the Church. Do you also see this, good Jesus, and does this rending not move you at all? Does so grievous a wound in your bride not wound you? If her unity so wounds your heart that you praise her, her disunity should so wound you that you pity her. The harmony of unity and uniformity moves you; let the dispersal of what was united move you.

Your locks have been parted and separated from one another, indeed against one another. Both sides boast that they hang from the neck of the bride and, boasting of their claim to her, try to tear others away from her. 'The Lord knows those who are his' and 'let everyone who calls on the name of the Lord depart from iniquity.'* Possessing this twin 'seal', as Paul calls it,* his bride remains steadfast amid the wicked hands of those who on all sides pluck and

2 Tm 2:19

1 Co 11:15

tear her apart. The kings of the earth and its princes have come together against Christ the Lord* and against his bride.   *Ps 2:2*

But the bride knows the Bridegroom, so that she follows not a stranger but her Lord. She does not fail to know herself, nor whose bride she is; therefore she refuses to desert or to depart for the flocks of her companions. Although they were her companions, they are such no longer. They have gone from us but they do not belong to us. How are they companions when they are not friends? For the friend of the Bridegroom stands and listens and with joy rejoices at his voice.* But the flocks do not listen or rejoice at the voice of the Bridegroom but rather at the voice of the Roman Emperor. Unless (and this we have more reason to admit) they do not so much rejoice as tremble at his roar. But 'the Lord knows those who are his', not those who belong to the Emperor. Therefore they cannot be moved at the roaring of the Lion* because they are held fast by the immovable seal of divine knowledge.   *Jn 3:29*   *Pr 19:12*

7. A good seal indeed is the knowledge of God, knowledge which is in accordance with his purpose, according to which the saints have been called.* Durable is this seal of his knowledge, because nothing will be effaced from it. Not only is nothing lost to it, but it gives birth to those who are to be saved, it predestines and stamps those it wishes to be its own.* It is a twofold seal, of divine purpose and human zeal, divine Providence and human devotedness. For concerning devotedness the apostle adds: 'And let everyone who calls upon the name of the Lord depart from iniquity.'*   *2 Tm 1:9*   *Rm 8:29*   *2 Tm 2:19*

Inspect the two parts of this seal: the one of divine grace only, the other both of grace and of liberty; the former of God's purpose, the latter of his assistance. His assistance directs the weak choice of our liberty; for his purpose disposes by predestining. In his purpose the Lord knows in his foresight those who are his own; in his assistance he makes this known to us. His purpose is the cause, his assistance its effect. His purpose is unchangeable, his assistance can be tested.* His purpose is the seal, his assistance its impression. His purpose is the root, his assistance its fruit; and by these fruits you will know those who call upon the name of the Lord.* For in his good pleasure he knows those who are his and plants them that they may produce this fruit in abundance. For this reason he says: 'Let everyone who calls upon the name of the Lord depart from iniquity'.* Let the man who claims that he belongs to the Lord not depart from unity. Nor can anyone depart of those whom divine knowledge has formed and strengthened.

In our text, not even a hair from the head of the Church will perish. For all these hairs have been numbered,* all have been clasped with the seal of predestining knowledge. This divine knowledge is irrevocable;* therefore the foundation stands firm, possessing the Lord's seal, the help of God's purpose and the efforts of our free will. The locks bound with this seal, no one will be able to tear from the head of the bride. In your hand, O Lord, are all the locks of the bride and no one will tear them from your hand. Hold fast, good Jesus, those whom you hold and gather again those whom you know; let him who knows himself to be yours, who says 'I belong to the Lord', who calls on the name of the Lord, depart from iniquity, approach the unity of the Church, the unity of head and body, that is let him be a hair of the neck and a hair united.

8. Nothing so wounds the heart of the Bridegroom, nothing so stirs his feelings and pierces his spirit as the unity of the bride, and that unity safeguarded and, as it were, strengthened amid the efforts of those who would disrupt it. Religious bishops abandon their own sees and fly from city to city to escape the persecutor. Men vowed to God, both clerics and monks, afflicted with tribulations and outrage, endure with joy the plundering of their goods, knowing that they have 'a better and enduring property',* in the unity of fraternal and ecclesiastical charity. For if a man gives the whole of his property for charity, 'he will look upon it as nothing'.*

Some indeed buy back with gifts the freedom of

ecclesiastical communion. It is a good buy but a disgraceful sale. Why do you sell what you yourself condemn? If you regard as schismatics those who have been separated from you, you should not have been induced by money to allow them licence for their error. If you regard it as schism, why continue to sell for gifts the liberty to practise it? But if the reality of ecclesiastical unity is with us, why do you try to disrupt it? If you occupy the throne of Peter by right of succession, why do you not maintain Peter's sentence upon those whom you consider schismatics? 'May your money', he says, 'go with you to perdition.'* Yet now you say: Let your money be saved for me, but let your soul go to perdition. For how is there not perdition where there is separation from the unity of the body? 'Let the babe be neither mine nor yours', said the woman, 'but let it be divided.'* So you even take money, since you cannot take souls.   *Ac 8:20*

1 K 3:26

Take what you take. Take gifts for yourself; leave souls to the Church. For she also seeks nothing but souls. But let them disperse to you their bodily goods, lest together with you they scatter the goods of the soul. For he who does not gather with the Church scatters. Quite significantly Christ says: 'He who does not gather with me scatters.'* For gathering implies a plan of unity as scattering suggests separation. The Church knows how to say with the Bridegroom: 'He who is not with me is against me.'* She leaves no middle course; either you gather with her or certainly you scatter; you are either with her or against her. Whereas (they claim) you are wont to say: If you do not wish to scatter with us, at least do not gather with them. If you are not with me, at least do not be against me. It is enough if you are neither for us nor for our adversaries.⁵   *Lk 11:23*

Mt 12:30

9. But that is not what Jesus, our Joshua, says: 'Are you for us or for our adversaries'?* He leaves no middle course. 'Is there no balm in Gilead', O good Jesus? Why therefore Lord, has the bruising of your bride not been healed?* Why has her wound, her swollen sore not been bound up, or treated with   *Jos 5:13*

Jr 8:22

medicine, or softened with oil?* Have you given your beloved, O Lord, enough of the vinegar of sorrow to drink?* When will you treat her with oil, your holy oil? The oil of the sinner, however, will not fatten her.

Even the opposition boast that they have oil. What else but oil do they continue to sell, while they flatter, promise honors and offer gifts? Their oil is not the healing of chrism but the rending of schism. So their oil is like their wine. Their words and their blows should be weighed in the same scale. My soul refuses to be consoled from the breasts of their consolation.* They have bared their breasts like jackals and at them suckle their whelps,* not the children of the Church.

For the Church has her own breasts. That is why in the encomium of the bride there follows immediately: 'How beautiful are your breasts, sister, my bride.' Recall, Lord Jesus, your children who are astray to the sweetness of this milk, that from the mouths of sucklings you may elicit praise when you have destroyed the foe and the victor.[6] Hasten then and exchange judgment for victory,* in order that those who call upon your name may dwell in unity, because in this unity you send blessing and life for ever and ever.* Amen.

Is 1:6
Ps 59:5

Ps 6:3; Is 66:11
Lm 4:3

Jb 23:7

Ps 132:3

NOTES ON SERMON THIRTY

1. G. writes to his brethren, *fratres,* in the second person plural throughout.
2. See *Cor Jesus: Commentationes in Litteras Encyclicas 'Haurietis aquas,'* ed. Augustinus Bea, Hugo Rahner, Henri Rondet, Friedr. Schwendimann (Rome: Herder, 1969). Bernard Leeming, in 'Consecration to the Sacred Heart' (I. 595-656), quotes from par. 1-2 in this sermon, and adds a useful bibliography on this devotion in England; Jean Leclercq, in 'Le Sacré Coeur dans la tradition bénédictine au moyen age' (II. 3-28), likewise refers to these paragraphs, and notes that G.'s comment on the bride's love, *non amat, sed redamat,* is found in Aelred of Rievaulx (*Sermones inediti,* ed. C.H. Talbot [Rome 1952] 40) *redamaret amantem,* and recur in the hymn of the Sacred Heart, *Quis non amatem redamet?* For the history of this devotion cf. A. Cabassut, 'Blessure d'amour,' in *DSp* (1937) 1727-1729, and a bibliography in *Heart of the Saviour: A Symposium on Devotion to the Sacred Heart,* ed. Josef Stierli (Freiburg im Br.: Herder, 1958). See also A. Hamon, 'Coeur Sacré', *DSp* 2 (1953) 1027: G. Dolan, 'Devotion to the Sacred Heart in mediaeval England,' in *Dublin Review* 120 (1897) 373-385.
3. Ep 4:13. See de Lubac, 1^2: 586, n. 5, 591, n. 7; 2^1:520, n. 5; 2^2:87, n. 1.
4. Migne, mss Paris 9605, Troyes 419: *et luminis et crinis;* Mab. omits second *et.*
5. I owe the following comment to my colleague, Dean Lawrence Desmond: 'Mabillon connects this passage to the schism of 1130. Yet in that incident no conflict occurred between Pope and Emperor, the latter indeed being one of the more devoted of Innocent II's adherents. Rather, this section 6 must be read along with section 8 which the learned Benedictine correctly interprets as having to do with the later struggle between Frederick Barbarossa and Pope Alexander. Because so many Cistercian colleagues were intimately involved in that context, Gilbert's adumbrations are of special interest. Cistercian abbots were present at the Council of Pavia but left hastily, when Victor was declared to be the legitimate pontiff. Others of the Order approached Frederick in Milan in an attempt to persuade him to withdraw his support of Victor. Subsequently, in General Chapter, the white monks declared in favor of Alexander III, an action which infuriated Frederick who, according to Helmhold, offered the monks of the Order in his realm the choice of either recognizing Victor or of being exiled. A systematic persecution was undertaken, the intensity of which historians have not agreed upon. The religious bishop alluded to by Gilbert may possibly be Conrad, bishop of Lubeck and a former monk of Clairvaux who was deposed by Frederick and fled to Clairvaux. Far from being intimidated other Cistercians were instrumental in preventing the Emperor from obtaining support in both England and France. The conclusion of the schism was mediated by Cistercian abbots

and the Emperor invited to submit to Alexander by way of Abbot Pons of Clairvaux. For a synthetic picture of the Cistercian rôle in the imperium at this time, see M. Preiss, *Die Politische, Tatigkeit und Stellung der Zisterzienser in Schisma 1159-1177* (Halle, 1934); S. Mitterer, "Die Cisterzienser und der Kirchenstreit zwischen Alexander III und Kaiser Frederick I", *Cisterzienserchronik* 34 (1922) 1-8, 21-26, 35-40.'

6. Unfortunately, we cannot date these paragraphs of G. on this schism in the Church. All the time G. was abbot, there was schism in the Church, and events described must have occurred in many places. Mabillon's note seems to require careful refining: *Non alius hic numero 8 pungi videtur, quam Alexander III, cui objectus fuit a Friderico imperatore antipapa Victor. Hunc auctor destructum cupit in fine sermonis, ubi 'ultorem' antea legebatur, non 'Victorem,' quae genuina lectio est ex dodice Vallis-Clarae.* See note 5 above.

7. Ps 8:3, reading *lactentium* for *lactantium*, (though the change from 'sucklings' to 'those who give suck,' would be in Gilbert's manner) and with Mabillon, *Victorem* for *ultorem*, the Anti-pope Victor IV, though *ultorem*, avenger, appears in the same verse of the Psalm, *ut destruas inimicum et ultorem;* mss Paris 9605, Troyes 419: *lactentium . . . victorem,* 'sucklings' and 'victor'.

SERMON 31

MILK FOR BABES

The bride offers material and spiritual milk for babes. 1-2. The bride experiences the ebb and flow of action and contemplation. 3. Teachers and prelates have twin breasts; kings and princes the left breast of temporal assistance; prelates and priests the right breast of consolation; religious prelates have both breasts. 4. The arts of women should be imitated in presenting the word of God. 5. The gentleness of the Gospel is more powerful than the harshness of the Law. Novatian and Pelagius are enemies of the grace of God. 6-7. How the gentleness of breasts are superior to the harshness of wine.

HOW BEAUTIFUL ARE YOUR BREASTS, SISTER, BETTER THAN WINE ARE YOUR BREASTS[1]*   *Sg 4:10*

Gently now we must touch upon the breasts of the bride. Though previously in more than one passage they have been drawn upon, still I know not whether their meaning has been fully expressed. Perhaps even touched upon lightly, they may yield us fresh nourishment. Who would not run avidly and with great expectation to the breasts which the Bridegroom has been at such pains to praise? These are the breasts from which Peter exhorts us to long for milk like newborn babes.* And does the present compliment not seem to amount to an invitation? 'How beautiful are your breasts, sister, my bride.' Praise so great was not poured out in a simple sentence without emphasis. The very manner of expression manifests the wonder and delight of the speaker.

But what is the reason for this order? Why, after the eye and the hair, does he turn at once to the breasts? Or why in her hair is unity praised and in her breasts their plurality? To me in the previous verse some transport of the mind and thought to God seems to be indicated, but in the present verse sobriety and temperance towards little ones. There one thing is necessary; here solicitude and teaching must be shared among many.* There the excess of fervent love, fixed on one target, well-aimed and penetrating, wounds the very breast of the Beloved; here temperate teaching and sober words fill little ones, as it were, with a drink of milk.

You see how no middle course is left in the eulogy of the bride, but with Paul she either flies beyond reason for God or bends down for our sake. 'Charity impels us', says Paul.* To what does it impel us? To ecstasy? No, not to ascend in ecstasy but to descend in charity. The former is the object of aspiration but the latter of service; there is the highest affection of one who knows no restraint but here is the highest affection of self-restraint. Good is the order indeed:² there to draw from the fountain and here to be drained; first to be inundated there and then to be emptied here; to be intoxicated there and here to intoxicate. Good is such an ebb and flow, if it be in

1 P 2:3

Lk 10:42, 2 Co 8:7

2 Co 5:13-14

moderation.

2. By your arrangement, O Lord, this alternation persists, the alternation of contemplation and consolation. Is he not blessed, every moment of whose life is spent either in inflicting on Christ wounds of charity or in offering breasts of devotion to his subjects? For my part, O Lord, whenever (if ever) intoxicated from the winecellar of your house, I seem to bring back from there distended breasts, they are drained by so many and such varied and painful current affairs that soon they are dried up, although previously they poured in abundance the milk of erudition and of grace. Happy is he who by some holy exchange sustains such zeal in himself that he may either penetrate, so to speak, into the very heart and consistory of wisdom or bring back thence breasts overflowing with the abundance of wisdom's delight.

She is clearly a bride who knows how to achieve such an alternation. Therefore in her praises, after the transport of contemplation, the breasts of consolation and doctrine are at once introduced: 'How beautiful are your breasts!' Pure is her eye and beautiful her breasts. Her eye belongs to the Bridegroom, her breasts to the children of the Bridegroom. Therefore her eye is spoken of in the singular, her breasts in the plural. For the temperature of the breasts must vary to satisfy the different characters they nourish. See how Paul for the Jews became a Jew, and for those outside the Law became as one outside the Law, and weak for the weak.* Does he not adapt as many breasts as he has disciples when he transforms himself into so many shapes? What else was his aim in such manifold changes of character but that his teaching might be instilled gently and like milk into the tender spirits of his hearers? He seems to abound in as many breasts as are the ways in which with ingenious art he adapted himself to the capacity of the weak. I became in your midst like a babe amid babes, he said, 'like a nurse taking care of her children'.*³

3. Now if you wish I shall point out for you the

1 Co 9:20-22

1 Th 2:7

two breasts of maternal piety. Indeed Paul himself points them out, when he says that 'piety is of value for everything, as it has' consolation 'for the present life and for the life to come'.* With these twin breasts the man who occupies the place of teacher and father in the Church must be endowed for the good of his subjects. With these breasts must he be equipped on right and left, that those who are entrusted to him may be given milk to drink and filled 'from the breasts of his consolation'.* Take one of these to be the left, the other the right: the left, assistance in temporal affairs; the right, in spiritual consolation: 'one who performs works of mercy with cheerfulness' and 'one who gives alms without guile'.* According to the prince of the apostles, the man who provides 'for the flock in his charge not under constraint but willingly',* offers the left breast, and the Church is promised in the prophecy of Isaiah that she will be suckled 'at the breast of kings'.* 'At the breast', says Isaiah, and not at the 'breasts', inasmuch as it is for kings to foster the Church principally with temporal goods, for this is her left breast, in which are 'riches and glory'.* About the right breast,[4] Paul teaches us, 'encourage the fainthearted',* and 'console such a one, lest he be overwhelmed by excessive sorrow',* and again 'you who are spiritual, should instruct' such a one 'in a spirit of gentleness'.* Now, speaking figuratively, some by their office have only the left breast, as those whom we mentioned above, kings and princes. On some it devolves by virtue of their office to offer mostly the right breast, as the Lord's priests and teachers, whose lips guard knowledge and from whom the law of the Lord is to be sought.* For these reap rather material benefits from the peoples subject to them, for whom they sow blessings of the spirit.*

But those who renounce all possessions, who bid farewell to temporal goods, who surrender themselves and all their possessions to a monastery and transfer completely to the jurisdiction of an abbot, reserving to themselves for the future no responsibility for themselves, they certainly are to be suckled

1 Tm 4:8; G.consolationem; promissionem Vulg.

Is 66:11

Rm 12:8

1 P 5:2

Is 60:16. Lam 7, n. 12.

Pr 3:16
1 Th 5:14

2 Co 2:7
Ga 6:1

Ml 2:7

1 Co 9:11

with the twin breasts of consolation.⁵ Therefore those who are in charge of such persons should not lack either breast, lest they seem to have a bosom multilated and maimed, reduced by deformity to a single breast. Those deprived of both breasts, however, hold this office in the Church both to their own injury and to the peril of others, lest perhaps the tongue of the suckling adhere to its palate* while his mother's breasts are dried up.* Obviously the praise given here to the bride is not meant for them: 'How beautiful are your breasts, sister, my bride.' Notice at the same time that not all breasts are beautiful, for 'praise is not beautiful on the lips of a sinner',* and in Proverbs: 'If sinners would suckle you, child, take no pleasure in them.'* See how the author not only refuses to recognize the breasts of some people as beautiful but is even ready to consider them suspect. Therefore he commends those of the bride, that you may know well to which you should safely have recourse.

Lm 4:4
Ho 9:14

Si 15:9

Pr 1:10

4. 'How beautiful are your breasts: better than wine are your breasts.' Two qualities the Bridegroom mentions in his praise of her breasts: beauty and excellence. Beauty suits the lover; excellence suits an infant. For what does it matter to an infant whether breasts are beautiful, provided they are breasts and overflow with wholesome milk? Their beauty then he recalls for his own sake and their blessing of milk for the sake of his children. Unless you have some better interpretation, apply their beauty to the charm of attractive behavior, and the rest of the eulogy of her breasts to instruction and erudition. Milk tastes sweeter to babes, when the nurse's life lends charm to the excellence of her teaching.

And if you wish to hear some spiritual and more developed interpretation of their beauty, I refer you to the devices of women, who cultivate and develop physical beauty and have mastered this art. For what are they more anxious to avoid in embellishing the bosom than that the breasts be overgrown or shapeless and flabby, or occupy the spaces of the bosom itself? Therefore they constrain overgrown and flabby breasts with brassieres, artfully remedying the shortcomings of nature. Beautiful indeed are breasts which are slightly prominent and are moderately distended; neither raised too much nor level with the bosom, as if pressed back but not pressed down, gently restrained but not hanging loose.

Following this model, let him who must utter good words, consoling words,[6] imitate the art and care of women. Let him adopt restrained language; let not the breasts of his words be sloppy or tumble out in disorder. Let them not replace rather than adorn, as it were, the bosom and consistory of the mind. Let them not have more bulk than grace, more flesh than milk. Let his discourse be pure and prudent, as occasion demands. Here let piety approach and observe the rhythm of beauty. Let the discourse not have more in the mouth than in the breast, lest the milk be spilt. The breasts should rise from the bosom and cling there; the bosom should not be merged into the breasts. From the abundance of the heart let the mouth speak;* let it speak from that abundance, not emptying itself entirely. The breasts must be restrained lest they spill over in excess.

Lk 6:45

You may see some people stumble into banalities, while they seek words of solace beyond what is right. While they wish to cheer an audience bored to death by long silence and glum from listlessness, through the wantonness of a capricious tongue they run on from useful comment to buffoonery and either before or after some grains of wheat they sow a great deal of cockle.* They speak to please and, as it is written, bake the bread of doctrine in laughter,* but a little while after the laughter they are without bread, without the bread of the saving word. The word of God is not to be adulterated,* or corrupted by an alien ingredient. Let it be satisfied with its own breasts, those of the two Testaments. Let these, learnt by heart, cling to your bosom; let them provide you with discourse full, as it were, of the milk of consolation; let them provide what others may imbibe. Let the Scriptures burst from the very roots of your bosom, that your message may not be affected but

Mt 13:25.
Lam 196, n. 173.
**Qo 10:19.*

2 Co 4:2

uttered with pure heartfelt affection, as Horace says: 'If you wish me to weep, you must first show me your tears.'* Let the affection of compassion and thanksgiving be born within you but let it flow through the words of sacred Scripture as through breasts to nourish your hearers. Let your feeling flow modestly as befits a serious topic, with petulance absent and serenity present. For it contributes to the beauty of the breasts if they rise a little and are slightly prominent, that they may have the required authority but no trace of austerity.

Ars Poetica 102-3

5. Therefore her breasts are said to be 'better than wine'. For so their praises continue immediately: 'better than wine are your breasts'. Breasts of grace, breasts of consolation, are better than the wine of austerity and harshness,[7] because they are more effective, better able to change sad and exasperated feelings, and to strengthen weak and tender feelings. They persuade more readily and encourage more gently, for 'a gentle word both mollifies enemies and multiplies friends'.* Gentle is the word of the Gospel; harsh is the word of the Law. Notice also how a gentle word changes the savage hearts of the Gentiles, transforming, as it were, briny salt waves into the flavor of milk. 'They shall drink the overflow of the sea like milk.'* This was said of the apostles under the figures of Zabulon and Issachar. Today who is tossed about in bitterness and disorder? Do not despair, offer your breasts, provide milk; perhaps tomorrow he himself will flow with milk. Who knows that a little drop will not change the whole mass? Yes, 'the Lord will give utterance with great power to those who proclaim good tidings'.* Barren and weak is the severity of the Law; it commands without grace and punishes without pardon; it lacks both breasts. It contains a foreshadowing of these breasts but it does not exhibit their reality. Remember that you are a minister not of the Law but of the Gospel, a minister of Jesus who in his passion rejected vinegar and at the Supper the sourness of the old wine.

Si 6:5

Dt 33:19

Ps 67:12

Novatian does not possess the breast of pardon nor Pelagius that of grace. Pelagius proclaims the blessings of a nature that has grown old and corrupt and claims that nature suffices for justification; Novatian denies the goodness of the divine nature while he rejects repentance. Pelagius, so to speak, recalls those who seek pardon, Novatian does not welcome the repentant. Pelagius drinks a toast to antiquity, Novatian to austerity. The teachings of Pelagius lack the freshness of the milk of grace; the teachings of Novatian its sweetness. 'In your sweetness', says the psalmist, 'you have prepared food for the poor man, O God.'* Pelagius is a rich man and does not need this sweetness; it is inborn in him, not prepared for him! Pelagius says, 'I have no need', and Novatian, 'I do not indulge'! The one is exceedingly rich, the other exceedingly harsh.[8]

Ps 67:11

Prepare, O Lord, prepare in your sweetness for your poor man, O God; do prepare, do repair, and only in your sweetness. Great is the abundance of sweetness which is imbibed from your breasts, O Lord. How often after serious excesses have I approached your breasts and pressed them insistently and what store of milk I have drawn from them, O Lord, you know! Where sin abounded, grace also abounded.* It was enough for me to reckon it as wealth if I but deserved pardon and behold there was also grace in plenty. I pressed one breast and both gave milk in abundance. Therefore your bride, drinking the milk of your grace and filled from the breasts of your consolation, has learned for her part also to offer her breasts rather than wine, for 'better than wine are her breasts'. Wine turns to vinegar with age; breasts pour out what is wholly new, wholly sweet. According to Scripture, 'fear is cast out' and 'charity never comes to an end'.* This is his new commandment, his ever fresh sweetness. Love cannot exist and fail to be sweet.

Rm 5:20

1 Jn 4:18; 1 Co 13:8

6. 'Better than wine' then 'are your breasts.' Wine is not bad, but breasts are better. Better indeed they are, yet they do not escape an admixture of wine. In the next chapter the Bridegroom will say: 'I have drunk wine with my milk.'* It were better, however, if one would drink milk alone and without

Sg 5:1

wine, for in wine there is terror, but in breasts the gentle wooing of compassion and grace. For although wine can be and usually is understood in a good sense, here in comparison with breasts wine seems to stand for something harsh and strong. Her breasts are better than wine, because gentle and fraternal compassion is better than the harsh and implacable feeling of an indignant spirit. Those who are 'without affection',* Paul describes as not having breasts. A bride who clings to her Bridegroom cannot have a human bosom deprived of the breasts of devotion. For to him belongs the breast-like mountain, the curdled mountain, the fertile mountain, the plump mountain.* How will the bride, whose resolve is to dwell on this mountain,* draw nothing from such an abundance of milk? And if we cannot yet dwell uninterruptedly on this mountain, let us return to it frequently, let us climb, let us be inebriated with breasts. For so Scripture has it: 'Let her breasts inebriate you at all times and in her love delight continuously.'* See to what meaning he turns his interpretation of breasts: to the inebriation and to the delights of love.⁹

Rm 1:31

Ps 67:16

Ps 67:17

Pr 5:19

7. What need is there to delay longer in seeking the purpose of breasts? Let us seek rather to be inebriated through them. For 'better than wine are breasts', because 'your mercy is better than life'.* Better is the affection of love than the affliction of the flesh and a drink of the milk of spiritual renewal is better than the wine of compunction.* In the wine harsh things are broached and tasted, until the old self is expelled and destroyed; in the milk, in the newness of life,* we draw milk from the wooing of divine kindness, a sign not of rout but of refuge. Good indeed is wine, but breasts are sweeter; good is compunction, but better is unction. 'For the fragrance of your ointments surpasses all perfumes.'* I see that your readiness to listen is now enkindled anew. Your appetite has been whetted by the fragrance of the bride's ointments. But through some immoderate hunger you desire this theme to be added today to that of the breasts; grant me a truce until morning. For today let the breasts suffice; tomorrow let us

Ps 62:4

Rm 7:6; Ps 59:5.
Lam 193, n. 154.

Rm 6:4

Sg 4:10

proceed to the ointments, if he grants fulfillment to our prayers who is both the eulogist and the donor of both breasts and ointments for his bride, Jesus Christ, who lives and reigns for ever and ever. Amen.

NOTES ON SERMON THIRTY-ONE

1.   G. addresses one individual throughout, except in the first sentence of par. 3, the last sentence of par. 6, and throughout par. 7. See Sg 1:1, 3, 12; 4:5, 10; 7:3, 7, 8, 12; 8:1, 8, 10. I am endebted to Denis Farkasfalvy of Our Lady of Dallas Abbey, Irving, Texas, for many suggestions in this sermon.
2.   Reading *ordo* for *odor*.
3.   See Ac 19:24-35; G. may be alluding to the many-breasted statues of Diana, and to the transformations of Proteus in Homer's *Odyssey*, 4:354-369.
4.   Reading *De dextra* for *Dextra* with Mab.
5.   RB 58:24-26. Lam 17, nn. 67, 68; 20 n. 84; Lam refers to RB cc. 1-2.
6.   Reading *consolatoria* for *spiritualia*, of some manuscripts; see 'the milk of consolation', par. 3, and 'the breasts of consolation', par. 5.
7.   Reading *duritiae* for *duritia*. Lam 7, n. 15.
8.   See *Church History*, Karl Bihlmeyer, rev. Hermann Tüchle, trans. V. E. Mills. (Westminster, Md.: Newman, 1958) I:166-8, Novatian; 281-4, Pelagius.
9.   Read *deflectat* with Flor. and Migne, for *delectat* of Mab. in last sentence of par. 6.

SERMON 32
THE FRAGRANCE OF THE ANOINTED

The bride is fragrant with the ointments of the Anointed. 1. The bride has an abundant store of ointments, though the funnel is too small for large receptacles. 2. Wine, breasts and ointments are compared mystically. 3. The flower of our flesh quickly wilts and festers. 4. We are anointed in baptism and in our hope of the resurrection. 5. A twofold ointment is impassibility and patience; fraternal love is an ointment preferable to prayer and sacrifice. 6. Charity is a twofold ointment, for God and for neighbor; without charity, other virtues have no perfume or fruit. 7. Mary's surpassing love changes from perfume to ointment. 8. Prayer is incense, but contemplative union is anointing.

BETTER THAN WINE ARE YOUR BREASTS AND THE FRAGRANCE OF YOUR OINTMENTS SURPASSES ALL PERFUMES*[1]   *Sg 4:10*

I have but a little oil and ointment, brothers, and today do you bring vessels so large and so empty? Do not be offended if I call your vessels empty. I do not mean to imply that they are dry but rather that they are capacious, inasmuch as your faculties are keen and receptive. Who has enough to fill such capacity? You are awaiting the ointments of the bride, waiting to see what store of perfumes she has, as if no attention should be paid to the funnel through which they must flow to you. Her store is indeed abundant but none the less consider the capacity of your servant. Be it as you will; I will not allege my incapacity lest you accuse me of failing to keep my word. I shall distill the little oil I have into your vast containers and may there be some Elisha to command, whose power may grant a good yield to our efforts.* And why not? Do not many Elishas sit here, many prophets or at least children of prophets? All these give orders. Even if they were inferior in merit, their very number could suffice to take the place of one great prophet.

I shall distill then something from what is left of the ointments. For they were poured out, you remember, sufficiently and in plenty at the beginning of the book, and perhaps they have not yet been drained to the dregs.* Now do I intend to draw off the dregs? Do not expect that of me, for I do not make so bold. There is a well-stocked store of ointments with the bride. There is no reason for you to say: drain it, empty it out to the bottom of her store.* Would that by accident I might be stuck in these dregs and not dip only my foot in the oil, as it was written of Asher.* Brothers, if we do not deserve to be plunged like the evangelist John into a cauldron of oil, into an abundance of ointments, if we do not deserve so plentiful an anointing, shall we despair of even a dip or at least of a scent? For only a scent is recommended here: 'And the fragrance of your ointments', says the Bridegroom, 'surpasses all perfumes.' Breasts serve to make you grow; ointments to secure you from fainting. 'Better than wine are your breasts and the fragrance of your ointments surpasses all perfumes.' And to link today's verse with yesterday's, let us say that breasts belong to the tender, ointments belong to the strong.

2. Let us compare these three, one with another: wine, breasts and ointments. In wine is the decline of the old man; in breasts the refreshment of the new man; in ointments a kind of delight. Through wine sensual perception is inebriated, lulled to sleep and

2 K 4:1-7

*Sg 1:3; Ps 74:9.
See Bernard,
SC 10:4; 12:1;
10; 13:8; 15:5.*

Ps 136:7

Dt 33:24.

overpowered; through the breast a new perception is nourished; through ointments an adult perception takes its delight. Through the first the old man is destroyed; through the second the new man is refreshed; through the third a man already approaching perfection is moved by ineffable joy. Is it not a good plan that you should advance from refreshment to delight, that after the firstfruits of milk you should advance to the delights of ointments? Even from the beginning of this Canticle both of these, ointments and breasts, have been recalled and linked together in eulogies of the bride.* No slight pleasure do they give him, since the Bridegroom reflects upon them so often in praise of his beloved, not being content to have mentioned them once. Do you not think he has been delighted by these praises which he reviews with such feeling and such frequency? *Sg 1:2-3*

There is something also you may apply to yourself from such care to repeat their praises; regard this repetition as an invitation to you. Do you also run in the fragrance of these ointments, or rather insure that they yield their fragrance in you that you also may be worthy to be told that 'the fragrance of your ointments surpasses all perfumes'. May you hear this verse not once only, but may the lips of your Beloved speak these praises to you again and again. Let the ointments in you be fresh and, as it were, ever new. Let them not dry up, or grow arid, or be emptied out. 'Oil poured out is the name' of the Beloved.* But see that it be poured out even unto you, not out of you. It is good if with the bride you may begin from ointments, but not good unless you end in ointments. Otherwise Paul asks of you: 'Having begun with the Spirit, are you now ending with the flesh?'* You are well anointed, if you are anointed with the Spirit. *Sg 1:2* *Ga 3:3*

Therefore be so anointed that your flesh may be changed through the oil. Let not the oil be changed or diminished through your flesh. Let neither the oil nor indeed the ointment depart from your head, but let it overflow and descend even to your feet, because in Christ Jesus both head and feet are not so much anointed as steeped in ointment. Let the oil enter into your interior, let it be drunk into your very affections, so that all that is carnal in you may be changed thanks to the oil. For a time will come when even the flesh will be changed thanks to the oil. One there was 'anointed' and steeped in 'the oil of gladness more than his fellows'.* He alone therefore was able to say before the time of his Resurrection: 'My flesh has been changed thanks to the oil.'* Rightly did the flesh which was exempt from carnality anticipate the hour of the general change. O desirable hour, 'O sweet anointing',* when and through which the flesh dissolved will ascend into incorruption! Yet before that state why should the flesh not descend into corruption?*

<small>Ps 44:8</small>

<small>Ps 103:24</small>

<small>Veni Creator Spiritus, 2nd stanza.</small>

<small>1 Co 15:42, 53.</small>

3. Yesterday you saw, brothers, you beheld with tears in your eyes, wretched flesh changed, flesh declining from corruptibility into corruption and declining indeed slowly enough and lingering unable to be wholly corrupted.[2] Corruption seemed to wish to possess by inheritance the body it had occupied and lest the body should cease to decay, corruption did not allow it to become wholly putrescent. Corruption restrained its powers as if unwilling to consume the substance quickly, that corruption might infect the flesh the longer. For when the flesh has been reduced to dust, what more can corruption do? 'All flesh is grass and all its glory like the flower of the field. The grass has withered and the flower has fallen.'* By these words the prophet expressed the immediacy of life's disappearance. He showed how easily the flesh, once blossoming like a flower with vital warmth, beautiful as the colors of the rose, but now plucked from the land of the living, withers suddenly indeed but does not fester so quickly. Therefore by comparing flesh with grass, he shows the rapidity of the sudden change but does not express the horror of slow and festering corruption.

<small>Is 40:6-7</small>

In that corpse you could see among the bones which had once been covered, some laid bare, some still not so much covered as defiled and wrapped in decay. In that pitiful flesh, corruption inched its slow way along and 'reaching from end to end mightily'* was destroying all parts without pity. I could also have said: it was disposing all parts of the flesh,* for destruction was obeying the nod of God who disposes of the flesh! A pitiful change but a beautiful plan, by which it pleased God that the glory of the flesh should be brought to dust only through decay. Let death rage, let corruption itself rage and riot against human flesh; let it ravage the flesh as much as it can, reduce it first to disease and then to ashes, for corruption can reduce to ashes the glory of the flesh, thus far and no further. Corruption cannot reduce to nothingness, nor utterly consume, nor possess in perpetuity, the glory of the flesh. 'Until the heavens are no more' the flesh 'will not rise'* but none the less then it will rise. For then the Lord will pour out from his Spirit upon all flesh.* Then the flesh of the saints will be changed thanks to the oil, because the Spirit of the Lord has anointed their flesh. Indeed we shall all rise again but we shall not all be changed.* *Ws 8:1* *Ws 8:1* *Jb 14:12* *Jl 2:28* *1 Co 15:51*

4. O how great is the power of that ointment, before the sight of which the yoke of so ancient a corruption will decay and the flesh which was consumed by tortures will return to the days of its youth, a youth which will not yield when another age succeeds. Wholly effective is the ointment through which so ancient a wound will be healed* and such a hoary decay will be changed into incorruptible health. This ointment is the property of the Church; therefore her children are called Christians after her Bridegroom Christ, whose name means 'the Anointed'. And we have already received this ointment at baptism.³ As there it produced sanctification, so also at the end of time it will produce that glorious change, when the flesh will be changed thanks to the oil. Who knows but that disease is meanwhile allowed to riot that from the violence of the disease may be shown the power of the remedy? *Ho 14:5*

Aptly therefore is the fragrance of this ointment commended, because though still from afar we sense its pleasing fragrance. To counteract any desolation which can affect the mind, what other antidote will you substitute as effective as unshakable hope in the resurrection to come and in that most blissful transformation? The teaching of the Gentiles does not include belief in the resurrection and the tradition of the Jews does not suggest its character. The former do not believe; the latter entertain an opinion incomplete and obscure concerning the spiritual glory of the resurrection and the ensuing resemblance to the angels. The Gentiles do not breathe the fragrance of this ointment; the Jews do not breathe it pure and clear but some other ointment in its place, one which is adulterated. With the Church alone the fragrance of this ointment exists pure and clear. So 'the fragrance of her ointments surpasses all perfumes'.

5. Good ointments are impassibility and patience. In virtue of the former the risen flesh will be incapable of injury; through the latter the devout mind remains uninjured amid provocation and insults. Through the former we possess by inheritance the land of our flesh with a quiet and unshaken right but through the latter we possess the soul itself. 'In your patience', says the Lord, 'you will possess your souls.'* What else is your patience but some fragrance of future impassibility? There no evils are inflicted, while here, thanks to your patience as to a soothing ointment, even evils inflicted are not felt. Altogether effective and useful is the ointment which amid assaults of the flesh both guards the soul from harm and supports it lest it weakens or falter or be overburdened.

Lk 21:19. Cornelius à Lapide, 8:69.

For my part I proclaim the usefulness of this ointment, while you perhaps seek its pleasure. I shall not be at a loss even here and 'shall show you a still more excellent' unction:* 'Count it all joy, brothers', says James, 'when you meet various trials.'* Does the man who knows how to rejoice in adversity not seem to you to be steeped in a more excellent ointment than the man who has learned not to be saddened in adversity? For the ointment by which sorrow is banned is inferior to that by which joy is encouraged. In Luke, the bride of Christ is bidden not only to

*1 Co 12:31
Jm 1:2*

tolerate her enemies but also to love them: 'Love your enemies.'* Good then are her ointments, for they wreathe the sad with gladness and envelop enemies with love. Yes, 'love is greater than all sacrifices and holocausts'.* Therefore 'the fragrance of your ointments excels all perfumes'.

Lk 6:35

Mk 12:33; G. holocaustomatibus: holocautomatibus, Vulg.

Good, of course, is the perfume of prayer and good is its incense; but hear what the Gospel prefers: 'If you are offering your gift at the altar', says the Lord, 'and there remember that your brother has something against you, leave your gift there before the altar and go first to be reconciled with your brother.'* You see plainly enough how the Lord prefers the ointment of reconciliation to the perfume of prayer. What is reconciliation but a repeated setting in harmony of discordant spirits? And about fraternal harmony and charity the Psalm tells you: 'See how good and how pleasant it is for brethren to dwell in unity.'* This is 'the more excellent way' of which Paul speaks* as greater than other spiritual gifts, greater than all perfumes. This ointment descends from the head 'to the beard' and 'to the hem of the robe'.* For Christ our Head first loved us in order that we might love him.*

Mt 5:23-24

Ps 132:1
1 Co 12:31; 13:1-13.

Ps 132:2
1 Jo 4:10

6. Therefore the bride also says she runs in the fragrance of unction, that is, in the rivalry of love. She does not say 'ointment' in the singular, but 'ointments' in the plural because love is twofold: one whereby we love him because he first loved us, the other whereby we love one another as he also loved us. We have from him the example and the gift of both loves. For he both shows the way of love and bestows the virtue of love. Therefore it is written: 'in the fragrance of his ointments we shall run.'* Do not the bond, the kindness[4] and the love of Father and Son and the mutual embrace of both through the Holy Spirit, envelop us with their pleasing fragrance and invite us to a kindred rivalry, that we also may be one as they are one?*

Sg 1:3

Jo 17:21

Happy indeed the man who follows and runs in the fragrance of that charity, that kindness, that love, that unction. For the Spirit himself, as it were, anoints through and through both of those whom he joins with so much sweetness of love. Let us imitate his unction, let us run in his fragrance. Fraternal charity is a rival and a kind of image of that divine and essential unity and, as it were, some reflection of that ointment and sweetness and mutual love. For 'see how good and how pleasant it is for brethren to live in unity'! It is 'like ointment on the head which descends' and so forth.* Now would that from our Head, which is above, some reflection of that ointment might fall upon us, that we also might deserve to be told that 'the fragrance of your ointments surpasses all perfumes'.

Review in your mind the other virtues; consider the value and the works of each; nothing in them breathes so sweet a fragrance as pure charity from the heart. What fragrance do fasts breathe for you or almsgiving, if the aroma of charity is absent from them? What sweet scent would even chastity itself and the endurance of sufferings waft your way, were they not rooted in charity? 'If I give my body to be burnt', says Paul, and if like burnt incense I wholly melt in the fire, 'but have not charity, it profits me nothing'.*[5] That cannot be freely accepted which is not offered with grace. Charity is the root; from charity the other virtues sprout like branches and therefore they must share its fruitfulness. Of what use is the branch of a good olive tree, if the fruitfulness and grace of its root does not thrive in the branch? So neither the virtues nor their works have any value, if the virtue of charity and love does not waft its fragrance through them.

7. What other perfume but love was breathed through Mary, whose name was mentioned recently in the Gospel? 'Many sins have been forgiven her', says the Lord, 'because she has loved much.'[6] Good is the fragrance of this ointment, for its grace wholly destroyed the stench of inveterate corruption and filled the whole house of the Church with pleasing sweetness. 'While the King was on his couch',* she broke a jar of pure nard and 'poured it out upon his head' as he reclined.[7] Now, that nard yielded and

still yields and will yield its fragrance to the end of the world. She set fire to good incense for Christ the Lord on the altar of her breast, as if her heart were ointment emptied out and melted by the flame of charity. When her Lord had been buried, see how dutifully, how assiduously she haunts his tomb. She comes and goes, sees the angels, summons the apostles, does not depart though they depart. My heart she says is aflame; I long to see my God; 'I seek and I do not find him'.* *Sg 3:1*

Does this anxious search of hers not seem to you to breathe a fragrance of rarest love? While these words are being chanted in her memory, are even the singers themselves not likewise set aflame? In the Gospel, even Jesus himself the object of her longing, scents the fragrance of her ointment and, as it were, runs toward her in the fragrance of passionate love. Why should he not hasten gladly to kindred ointments? As if in the early morning he hastens to her and 'rising at dawn on the first day of the week he appears first to Mary',* and anoints her 'with the oil of gladness beyond her fellows',* showing her that he was already risen in glory. Now he changes her perfume into ointments and transforms her desires into delight. *Mk 16:9* *Ps 44:18*

8. The man who prays and desires seems to me to offer perfume. But he is then steeped in ointment when he gains access to the one he loves and takes delight in his presence. It is good indeed to pray and to long for the Lord but to love him and hold him and enjoy him is better. And, so to speak, when you have nothing it is good to beg but it is better to eat. If you can love someone in his absence, how much more when he is present, when he grants you his company, when sweet experience serves food for love. Then indeed the soul is anointed more spiritually and more profusely when it is more closely joined with him who has been anointed with spirit and power.* Then especially the soul pleases the Beloved and breathes forth a sweeter fragrance, when it has been wholly poured into him, when clinging to him it is fragrant with the ointment of union, with *Ac 10:38. Lam 157-8, and n. 28*

that ointment which overflows from the Bridegroom to the bride.

Pleasant altogether and sweet is the scent of this dwelling together into one, 'like ointment on the head, which descends', and so forth.* Therefore 'the fragrance of her ointments surpasses all perfumes'. And if the bride herself possesses other ointments, none are like that which descends upon her especially at this hour when she clings to her Beloved, when she lingers between his breasts, when she lies in the consistory of his heart. In our Canticle, 'when the king is on his couch',* then the bride's nard wafts its fragrance, a good fragrance surpassing all perfumes, the fragrance of the Bridegroom, or rather the fragrance which is the Bridegroom. For he is the ointment of his beloved, he is her fragrance, for he takes pleasure for his own sake in his beloved, he diffuses his fragrance through her. And may this ointment not depart from our head and may the incense of its fragrance ascend from our hearts for ever and ever. Amen.

Ps 132:1-2

Sg 1:11

NOTES TO SERMON THIRTY-TWO

1. G. addresses one individual, except in par. 1, in the first sentence of par. 2, and in the first sentence of par. 3.
2. With par. 3, compare Roger's letter, Ro 15.
3. See Jacques Guillet, 'Esprit saint', *DSp* 4 (1961) 1253-4.
4. Reading *suavitas* for *suavitatis,* with Mab. Lam 16, n. 60.
5. Read *gratis suscipi* with Migne.
6. Lk 7:37, 47: Vulg. *remittuntur;* G. *dimissa sunt,* a verb also in Lk 7:47, 49. Lk leaves this *peccatrix* nameless; Jn 12:3 in a parallel, names Mary of Bethany. G. conflates texts concerning Mary the sinner, Mary of Bethany, and Mary of Magdala, for par. 7. The next sermon, S 33, was delivered on an Easter Sunday; hence one might suppose that S 32 was given on the Thursday after Palm Sunday, when Lk 7:36-40 was read, or even on Easter Monday when Jn 12:1-8 was read. But Lk 7:36-40 was also read on July 22, the Feast of Mary Magdalene, and liturgists among the monks at *Notre Dame des Prairies,* Manitoba, assure me that many of Gilbert's reflections are redolent of texts in the Mass and Office of this Feast. The 2nd nocturn for the feast is from Gregory the Great, *In Evan. Hom.* 25:1-2; PL 76:1189-90: *Quae a monumento Domini, etiam discipulis recedentibus, non recedebat; exquirebat, quem non invenerat; flebat inquirendo, et amoris sui igne succensa, ejus quem ablatum credidit, ardebat desiderio.* 'Her anxious search' is appropriate; indeed the classical passage in the Canticle was the lesson at Vigils, Sg 3:1-4, and the epistle at the Mass for the Feast, Sg 3:2-5, and 8:6-7. 'In her memory', Mt 26:3 and Mk 14:9, would be appropriate for the Feast of Mary Magdalene. 'Set aflame' is a reminiscence of Sg 8:6, the fourth lesson of the Feast. Whenever the sermon was given, G. seems in its preparation to have had in mind the liturgy for the Feast of Mary Magdalene.
7. *nardi pistici,* Jo 12:3; *super caput,* Mt 26:7, Mk 14:3.

ABBREVIATIONS

ABR   *American Benedictine Review.* Newark, New Jersey, 1950-.
ASOC   *Analecta Sacri Ordinis Cisterciensis; Analecta Cisterciensia.* Rome, 1945-.
CC   Corpus Christianorum series. Turnhout, Belgium, 1953-.
CF   Cistercian Fathers Series. Spencer, Mass., Washington, D.C., Kalamazoo, Mich., Cistercian Publications, 1970-.
CS   Cistercian Studies Series. Spencer, Mass., Washington, D.C., Kalamazoo, Mich., Cistercian Publications, 1969-.
CSt   *Cistercian Studies.* Chimay, Belgium, 1961-.
Cîteaux   *Cîteaux: Commentarii cistercienses; Cîteaux in de Nederlanden.* Westmalle, Belgium, 1950-.
Coll.   *Collectanea o.c.r.; Collectanea cisterciensia.* Rome, 1934-.
de Lubac   De Lubac, Henri, *Exégèse Médiéval.* Paris, Aubier, 1959-64.
DSp   *Dictionnaire de Spiritualité,* Paris, 1932-.
Dion   *Oeuvres Complètes de Saint Bernard,* V:1-319, Latin text and French tr. of Gilbert of Hoyland, P. Dion. Paris: Vivès, 1873.
E   Epistle of Gilbert of Hoyland, cited by number and paragraph.
Flor.   *Sermones super Cantica Canticorum, Editio princeps* [of Gilbert of Hoyland]. Florence, Nicolaus Laurenti, 1485.
G.   Gilbert of Hoyland.
Gilson   Gilson, Etienne, *The Mystical Theology of Saint Bernard,* tr. A. H. C. Downes. London: Sheed and Ward, 1940.
Lam   M. Jean Vuong-dinh Lam, 'Le Monastère: Foyer de Vie Spirituelle d'après Gilbert de Hoyland' and 'Les observances monastiques: instruments de Vie Spirituelle d'après Gilbert de Hoyland', Coll. 26 (1964) 5-21, 169-199.
Leclercq   Leclercq, Jean, *The Love of Learning and the Desire for God: a study of monastic culture,* N.Y.: Fordham Press, 1961.

Miquel   Miquel, Pierre, 'Les Caractères de l'expérience religieuse d'après Gilbert de Hoyland', Coll. 27 (1965) 150-159.
Morson   Morson, John, 'The English Cistercians and the Bestiary', *Bulletin of John Rylands Library* 39 (1956) 146-172.
MS   *Mediaeval Studies.* Toronto, 1939-.
R.   Roger of Byland, 'Lac Parvulorum', ASOC 7 (1951) 218-231.
RAM   *Revue d'Ascétique et de Mystique.* Toulouse, 1920-.
RB   *St. Benedict's Rule for Monasteries.* Tr. Leonard Doyle, Collegeville: Liturgical Press, 1948. *La règle de S. Benoît.* Sources chrétiennes 181-183, ed. Adalbert de Vogüé (1972).
R. Ben.   *Revue Bénédictine.* Maredsous, Belgium, 1899-1910; 1911-.
S   Gilbert of Hoyland, *Sermons on the Canticle,* cited by number and paragraph.
SAn   *Studia Anselmiana* series. Rome, 1933-.
SBOp   *Sancti Bernardi Opera,* ed. J. Leclercq, C. H. Talbot, H. M. Rochais. Rome: Editiones Cistercienses, 1957-.
SC   Bernard of Clairvaux, *Sermons on the Song of Songs.* SBOp 1-2, tr. Kilian Walsh, The Works of Bernard of Clairvaux, CF 4, 7, [31, 40].
SMC   *Studies in Medieval Culture.* Kalamazoo, Mich., 1964-.
T   Gilbert of Hoyland, Ascetical Treatise, cited by number and paragraph.
Talbot   Talbot, C. H., 'A Letter of Roger, Abbot of Byland', ASOC 7 (1951) 218-231.
VCH   *The Victoria History of the Counties of England,* ed. William Page. II, *A History of Lincolnshire,* 22. The Abbey of Swineshead, pp. 145-46.
Vulg.   Vulgate.
White   White, Terence Hanbury, *The English Bestiary.* New York: Putnam, 1960.

Psalms have been cited according to the Vulgate enumeration. Abbreviations and nomenclature conform to that of the Jerusalem Bible.

A SELECTED BIBLIOGRAPHY

A Lapide, Cornelius. *Commentaria in Scripturam Sacram*, re-ed., Augustine Crampon. Paris: Vivès, 1860.
Blaise, Albert. *Corpus Christianorum Continuatio Medieualis, Lexicon Latinitatus Medii Aevi.* Turnhout: Brepols, 1975.
Bouyer, Louis. *The Cistercian Heritage,* tr. Elizabeth A. Livingstone, Westminister, Md.: Newman, 1958.
Buhot, Jacqueline. 'L'Abbaye Normande de Savigny'. *Moyen Age,* 46 (1936) 1-19, 104-121, 178-190, 249-272.
Cabussut, A., Olphe-Gaillard M., 'Cantique des cantiques au Moyen Age.' DSp 2 (1953) 101-102.
—— 'Une dévotion médiévale peu connue: la dévotion à Jésus notre Mère'. RAM 25 (1949) 234-245.
Chatillon, Jean. 'Cordis Affectus au Moyen Age'. DSp 2 (1953) 2287-2300.
—— 'Hic, ibi, interim'. RAM (1949) 194-199.
Cheney, C.R. 'Les Bibliothèques cisterciennes en Angleterre au XIIe siècle'. *Mélanges de Saint Bernard.* Dijon (1953) 375-382.
Chenu, M.D. *La théologie au douzième siècle.* Paris, 1957.
Cloes, H. 'La systematisation théologique pendant la 1ère moitié de XIIe siècle'. *Ephemerides Theologicae* 34 (1958) 277-328.
Colombas, G.M. 'Paradis et vie angélique, Le sens eschatologique de la vocation chrétienne'. *Spiritualité monastique.* Paris, 1961.
Costello, Hilary, 'Gilbert of Hoyland'. *Cîteaux* 27 (1976) 109-121.
Déchanet, J.M. 'Amor ipse intellectus est'. *Revue du Moyen Age Latin* 1 (1945) 349-374.
—— 'La contemplation au XIIé siècle'. DSp 2 (1953) 1948-66.
—— 'Les fondements et les bases de la spiritualité bernardine'. *Cîteaux* 4 (1953) 292-313.
De Clerck, E. 'Droits du démon et nécessité de la Rédemption'. RTAM 14 (1947) 32-64.

─── 'Questions de sotériologie médiévale'. RTAM 13 (1946) 150-184.
Delatte, Paul. *The Rule of Saint Benedict,* tr. Justin McCann. London: Burns and Oates, 1921.
Delfgaauw, P. 'An approach to saint Bernard's sermons on the Song of songs'. Coll. 23 (1961) 148-161.
─── 'La lumière de la charité chez S. Bernard'. Coll. 18 (1956), 42-69, 306-320.
De Lubac, H. *Exégèse médiévale: Les quatre sens de l'Ecriture.* Paris: Aubier, Coll. *'Théologie',* 1959-64.
Didier, J.C. 'L'ascension mystique et l'union mystique par l'Humanité du Christ selon saint Bernard.' *La vie spirituelle, Supplément* 5 (1930) 140-155.
Dimier, A. 'Les concepts de moine et de vie monastique chez les premiers Cisterciens'. *Studia Monastica* 1 (1959) 399-418.
─── 'Ménagerie Cistercienne' and 'Héraldique Cistercienne'. *Cîteaux* 24 (1973) 5-30, 267-282.
─── 'Observances monastiques'. ASOC 11 (1955) 149-198.
Dugdale, G. *Monasticon Anglicanum.* London: 1846-1855.
Dumeige, Gervais. 'Dissemblance'. DSp 3 (1957) 1330-43.
Dumont, C. 'L'équilibre humain de la vie cistercienne d'après le bienheureux Aelred de Rievaulx'. Coll. 18 (1956) 177-189.
Dumontier, M. *Saint Bernard et la Bible.* Paris, 1953.
Foreville, Raymonde, 'Gilbert de Sempringham'. DSp 6 (1967) 374-375.
Gilson, Etienne, *The Christian Philosophy of Saint Augustine,* tr. L.E.M. Lynch. London: Gollancz, 1961.
─── *History of Christian Philosophy in the Middle Ages.* New York: Random House, 1954.
─── *The Mystical Theology of Saint Bernard.* Tr. A. H. C. Downes. London: Sheed and Ward, 1955.
Hallam, H. E. *Settlement and Society.* Cambridge U. Press, 1965.
Hallier, Amédée. *The Monastic Theology of Aelred of Rievaulx,* tr. Columban Heaney, CS2. Spencer, Mass., 1969.
Hill, Bennet D. *English Cistercian Monasteries and their patrons in the Twelfth Century.* Urbana: U. of Illinois Press, 1968.
Histoire Littéraire de la France. Edd. Benedictines of St. Maur and L'Institut des Inscriptions et Belles Lettres. Paris: Imprimerie Nationale, 1733-19--; 'Gilbert de Hoylandia', 13 (1814) 461-69.
Ioannis de Forda. *Super extremam partem cantici canticorum sermones CXX,* edd. Edmond Mikkers and H. Costello. *CC Continuatio Mediaeualis* 17-18. Turnhout: Brepols, 1970.
Javelet, Robert, 'Contemplation et vie contemplative aux VIe-XIIe siècles'. DSp 2 (1953) 1929-1948.

───── 'Exercises spirituels dans le Haut Moyen Age'. DSp 4 (1961) 1905-1908.

───── 'L'extase chez les spirituels du XIIe siècle'. DSp 4 (1961) 2113-2120.

───── 'Image et Ressemblance aux 11e et 12e siècles'. DSp 7 (1971) 1425-1434.

───── 'Intelligence et amour chez les auteurs spirituels du XIIe siècle'. RAM 37 (1961) 273-290, 429-450.

───── *Psychologie des auteurs spirituels du XIIe siècle*. Strassbourg 1959.

───── *Saint Bernard mystique*. Paris, 1948.

Knowles, David. *The English Mystical Tradition*. New York: Harper Torchbook, 1961.

───── *The Episcopal Colleagues of Archbishop Thomas à Becket*. Cambridge University Press, 1951.

───── *The Monastic Order in England*. Cambridge University Press, 1950.

───── *The Nature of Mysticism*. New York: Hawthorne, 1966.

───── *The Religious Orders in England*, 3 vols. Cambridge University Press, 1950.

Knowles, David, C.N.K. Brooke, Vera C.M. London, *The Heads of Religious Houses: England and Wales, 940-1216*. Cambridge U. Press, 1972.

Knowles, David and R. Neville Hadcock. *Medieval Religious Houses in England and Wales*. New York: Longmans, Green, 1953.

Knowles, David, and J.K.S. St. Joseph. *Monastic Sites from the Air*. Cambridge University Press, 1952.

Lambert, M. 'La date de l'affiliation de Savigny et de la Trappe à l'Ordre de Cîteaux'. Coll. 3 (1936) 231-233.

Lebreton, M. 'Christ and the christian faith according to St. Bernard'. *Cîteaux* 12 (1961) 105-119.

───── 'Recherches sur les principaux thèmes théologiques traités dans les sermons du XIIè siècle'. RTAM 23 (1956) 5-18.

Leclercq, Jean. 'Disciplina'. DSp 3 (1957) 1291-1302.

───── 'Les écrits de Geoffroy d'Auxerre, Appendices, II: La première rédaction des Sermones in Cantica de Gilbert de Hoyland'. *Revue Bénédictine* 62 (1952) 289-290.

───── 'Ecrits monastiques sur la Bible aux XIe–XIIIe siècles'. MS 15 (1953) 95-106.

───── 'Etudes sur le vocabulaire monastique du moyen âge', SAn 48 (1961).

───── 'Le genre épistolaire au moyen âge'. *Revue du Moyen Age latin,*

2 (1955).

——— *The Love of Learning and the Desire of God,* tr. Catherine Misrahi. New York: Fordham University Press, 1961.

——— 'Monachisme et pérégrination du IXe au XIIe siècle'. *Studia Monastica* 3 (1961) 33-52.

——— *Otia Monastica.* SAn 51 (1963).

Leclercq, Jean, François Vandenbroucke, Louis Bouyer. *The Spirituality of the Middle Ages.* London: Burns and Oates, 1968.

Lekai, Louis. *The White Monks.* Our Lady of Spring Bank, Okauchee. Wis.: Cistercians, 1953.

——— *The Cistercians: Ideals and Reality.* Kent, Ohio: Kent State Univ. Press, 1977.

Loomis, Roger Sherman. *The Grail, from Celtic Myth to Christian Symbol.* New York: Columbia U. Press, 1963.

Marié, G. 'Familiarité avec Dieu, Courant bénédictin et cistercien'. DS 5 (1962) 50-53.

Manrique, A. *Annales Cistercienses,* 4 vols. Lyons, 1642-1649.

Merton, L. 'Action and contemplation in St. Bernard', Coll. 15 (1953) 26-31, 203-216; 16 (1954) 105-121.

——— 'La doctrine de l'image chez saint Bernard'. *Ephemerides Theologicae* 23 (1947) 70-129.

——— 'Le principe de l'ordination dans la théologie spirituelle de S. Bernard'. Coll. 8 (1946) 178-216.

Mikkers, E. 'De vita et operibus Gilbert de Hoylandia'. *Cîteaux* 14 (1963) 33-43, 265-279.

——— 'Les sermons inédits de Jean de Ford sur le Cantique des cantiques'. Coll. 5 (1938) 250-261.

Miquel, Pierre. 'Les Caractères de l'Expérience Religieuse d'après Gilbert de Hoyland'. Coll. 27 (1965) 150-159.

Morson, John. 'The English Cistercians and the Bestiary'. *Bulletin of the John Rylands Library* 39 (1956) 146-170.

Migne, J.P., ed. *Patrologia Graeca.* Paris: 161 vols., 1857-1876. The volume number precedes the colon; the column number follows it.

——— *Patrologia Latina.* Paris: 222 vols., 1841-1864. The volume number precedes the colon; the column number follows it.

Prayers and Meditations of St. Anselm, tr. Benedicta Ward. Harmondsworth: Penguin, 1973.

Le règle de saint Benoît. Sources chrétiennes 181-183. Ed. Adalbert de Vogüé. Paris: Cerf, 1972.

Reypens, Leonce. 'Connaissance mystique de Dieu, au 12e et 13e siècles.' DSp 3 (1957) 829-901.

Riedlinger, H. 'Gilbert v. Hoyland.' *Lexikon für Theologie und Kirche,*

B. IV (1960) 890.

Robert, A., Tournay, R., Feuillet, A. *Le cantique des Cantiques*. Paris: Gabalda, 1963.

The Rule of Saint Benedict. Edited by Justin McCann. London: Burns Oates, 1952.

St. Benedict's Rule for Monasteries. Tr. Leonard Doyle, Collegeville: Liturgical Press, 1948.

Sancti Bernardi Opera, edd. J. Leclercq, C.H. Talbot, H.M. Rochais. Rome: Editions Cistercienses, 1957-.

Sancti Bernardi Opera Omnia, ed. Jean Mabillon. Milan: Gnocchi, 1690, rpt. 1850-52.

Smalley, Beryl. *The Study of the Bible in the Middle Ages*. Oxford, 1952, 2nd ed.

Squire, Aelred. *Aelred of Rievaulx: a study*. London, SPCK, 1969.

Talbot, C.H. 'A Letter of Roger, Abbot of Byland'. ASOC 7 (1951) 219-221.

Valléry-Radot, Irénée. 'La Queste del Saint Graal'. Coll. 17 (1956) 3-20, 199-213, 321-332.

Van den Bosch, Amatus. 'Intelligence de la Foi chez Saint Bernard'. *Cîteaux* 8 (1957) 85-108.

Vandenbroucke, François. 'Direction spirituelle en Occident, au Moyen Age'. DSp 3 (1957) 1083-1098.

Vuong-dinh-Lam, M. Jean. *Doctrine Spirituelle de Gilbert de Hoyland, d'après son Commentaire sur le Cantique des cantiques*. Diss., Rome: Collegium Anselmeanum, 1963.

—— 'Le Monastère: foyer de vie spirituelle d'après Gilbert de Hoyland', Coll. 26 (1964) 5-21.

—— 'Les Observances Monastiques: instruments de vie spirituelle d'après Gilbert de Hoyland', Coll. 26 (1964) 169-199.

—— 'Gilbert de Hoyland', DSp 6 (1967) 371-374.

White, Terence Hanbury. *The English Bestiary*. New York: Putnam, 1960.

William of St Thierry. *Exposition on the Song of Songs*. CF 6. Spencer, Mass., 1970.

www.ingramcontent.com/pod-product-compliance
Lightning Source LLC
Chambersburg PA
CBHW032036290426
44110CB00012B/826